WATCHING
THE DETECTIVES

WATCHING
THE DETECTIVES

Deborah Locke

ABC
Books

The ABC 'Wave' device is a trademark of the Australian Broadcasting Corporation and is used under licence by HarperCollins*Publishers* Australia.

This edition first published in 2003 by ABC Books for the Australian Broadcasting Corporation.
This edition by HarperCollins*Publishers* Australia Pty Limited
ABN 36 009 913 517
harpercollins.com.au

HarperCollins*Publishers*
25 Ryde Road, Pymble, Sydney, NSW 2073, Australia
31 View Road, Glenfield, Auckland 0627, New Zealand
A 53, Sector 57, Noida, UP, India
77–85 Fulham Palace Road, London, W6 8JB, United Kingdom
2 Bloor Street East, 20th floor, Toronto, Ontario M4W 1A8, Canada
10 East 53rd Street, New York NY 10022, USA

National Library of Australia Cataloguing-in-Publication data

Locke, Deborah Lee.
    Watching the detectives / Deborah Locke.
    ISBN: 978 0 7333 2796 4 (pbk.)
    Locke, Deborah Lee.
    New South Wales. Police – History.
    Policewomen – New South Wales – Biography.
    Police corruption – New South Wales.
    Australian Broadcasting Corporation.
363.2092

Cover design by Jane Waterhouse
Cover images courtesy of shutterstock.com
Typeset in 10.5 on 16pt Sabon by Kirby Jones
Printed and bound in Australia by Griffin Press
70gsm Classic used by HarperCollins*Publishers* is a natural, recyclable product made from wood grown in sustainable forests. The manufacturing processes conform to the environmental regulations in the country of origin, Finland.

7 6 5 4 3   10 11 12

*To my darling husband Greg
and our three beautiful children
Vanessa, Hayes and Bronte*

ACKNOWLEDGMENTS

I'd like to thank the following people from my time in the New South Wales Police: former Assistant Commissioner Christine Nixon who was always friendly, supportive and a great role model for all policewomen; former Detective Inspector Michael Drury who helped me through a tough period of my career and who gave me shelter from the storm; former Detective Sergeant Kimbal Cook for his honesty, strength, integrity and determination; Detective Inspector Bruce Van Der Graaf who was a friend to Greg and me when most people were afraid to be associated with us.

I am grateful to John Hatton for his lifelong service to others and for his relentless pursuit of the corrupt in public office. When I came up against brick walls in telling my story, he was instrumental in breaking them down. I would also like to acknowledge former journalist Morgan Og as a person whom I trusted and who was always prepared to report the truth about the New South Wales Police Force.

Thanks also to: my doctor Jean Lennane, the president of Whistleblowers Australia, who has supported me on a regular basis for the last decade and without whom I would not be standing; Megan Taylor for her patience, good humour and the ability to bring me back from the edge; Dr Keith Hartman for his skill, kindness and ability to listen; Dr Anthony Santamaria who cared for our family and gave me emotional support when we lived in Balmain; Dr Bobby Kumar who, apart from being a great GP, loves to hear my stories about the cops and who also has a few of his own; Dr Albert Mansour, who has worked wonders with our son Hayes; my legal team of Mark Turner and Lee Poulson of Messrs Jones, Staff and Co for their strength and kindness and Susan Davitt from Redfern Legal Centre.

My deepest thanks to Jenny Reid who came to help us from the Benevolent Society when Bronte was born and has remained a true friend; Kate Goodyer who became a great friend to Hayes and taught him to communicate with the outside world; Marion Thomas, whose support helps keep our family going. Special thanks to Rev Ivan Ransom who was always available in times of crisis and celebrations as well. His talents extend well beyond the spiritual.

For their advice, support and encouragement I wish to thank: Annette Hughes and Rose Creswell from the Cameron Creswell Agency; Graham Bates and Justine Munsie from Mallesons Stephen Jaques; and Stuart Neal, Angelo Loukakis, Jacqueline Kent and Jane Finemore from ABC Books, without whose help this book would not have been possible.

Finally I thank my husband for being strong enough to stand by me when I took on the NSW Police and many people were telling him to run. Greg's honesty and integrity are what first attracted me to him. Many people didn't think our marriage could survive, but here we are eleven years down the track and still going strong. His belief that this story should be told gave me the inspiration to sit down to the keyboard and get started.

Deborah Locke
Sydney 2003

CONTENTS

A BIG LUNCH

Ron was as flash as a rat with a gold tooth. He always wore large gold rings and the latest in men's fashion. With his dark hair cut very short, he professed to be of Polish heritage, but I suspected he was really Russian or Hungarian.

It was a morning late in 1988. I came into the office to find Ron jumping out of his skin with excitement. I had never seen him so cheerful. "It's the big time today," he said smiling. "I'll show you what it's all about, being a detective. We have a big lunch on today, and if you're a good little girl I'll let you come."

He was almost prancing when he walked, which I found very amusing. *Oh, this will be good,* I thought. *This is going to be just another piss-up.* Little did I know.

Ron had been counting down to midday all morning. He snatched the keys to our unmarked car from on top of my desk. He was going to drive. He told me we were going to a very classy local Chinese restaurant; I had never eaten there before. We grabbed our coats, left the office and walked out the back to a fenced car park adjoining Parramatta police station. Before long we were entering the car park of the restaurant. Intelligence reports indicated that at one time it had been an illegal gaming den. As Ron parked the car against the wall, I noticed two other unmarked police vehicles.

The restaurant was fairly large, with the usual gold dragons, bamboo pots, fish tank, and paper lanterns hanging from the ceiling. *This will be good*, I thought. *Cool, a long lunch. Ron's obviously found a new restaurant owner to impress.*

Smiling, the man on the door directed us to where an Asian man was seated at a large round table near the back of the room. Although seated I could see he was uncommonly tall and thin, wearing an immaculate dark suit. A colleague of Ron's was also seated at the table. His face fell when he saw me. He leaned over towards Ron as we sat down, and said, "What did you bring *her* for?" not caring whether I heard him or not.

"Oh she's all right," said Ron.

"Is she?"

"You can trust her. She'll be all right. I'm training her."

Slowly other characters started to roll in. It wasn't long before I had a feeling there was something more going on than just a big lunch. Two very distinguished-looking lunch guests wearing suits were introduced as owning a used car yard. They appeared to be treated as special guests. The next to arrive were four city detectives from one of the squads. They were casually dressed in jeans and polo shirts, not suits like the divisional detectives. I had never seen them before, and I haven't since.

Things were progressing in a jovial atmosphere with abundant Crown lagers. Combination chow mein, sweet and sour pork kept rolling in. Over time the table was covered in double-shot glasses of scotch and palate-cleansing ales. In those days my preference alternated between gin and tonic and Malibu and dry.

Dressed as always in a black or dark grey suit with white shirt and thin dark tie was Louis Bayeh. Well known in police circles, Bayeh was also a Parramatta celebrity. I had met him before; he had asked me to approach one of my close relatives to be a front man for him at a well-known disco. I was getting used to everyone's blatant disrespect towards me as a woman, from police to crooks, but I didn't understand why the cops were so buddy-buddy with the baddies.

This is going to be big, I thought, and my hunch was confirmed when Detective Sergeant Roger Rogerson joined the group. Suddenly things didn't look so good, and I started to feel as if I was well and truly in the wrong place. I had thought the cops were just pretending to be mates with these guys to get a brief on them, the sort of thing I had been used to in undercover work. It was starting to dawn on me that the relationship here between cops and crims was different.

I couldn't decide whether to leave or not, and I didn't want to draw attention to myself by getting up in the middle of lunch. Convention dictated that I shouldn't leave until Ron had finished. I was definitely not meant to be there that day and my neck had begun turning red, always a giveaway.

I had no idea what was going to happen. Because I was also young and good-looking, were they going to get really drunk and hand me over to someone as a sexual offering? I had come from the Gaming Squad, so maybe they thought I looked like recruitable material. I was the only woman present and I was scared; being with drunken coppers was not safe. As I had another gin to calm my nerves, it crossed my mind that if Internal Affairs were videoing the whole thing, my career would be down the toilet.

The meeting developed a definite pattern. Whenever any of the players needed to talk business, they would quietly get up and move to another table in the restaurant, out of hearing. This continued all afternoon. Louis or Roger always seemed to have someone away in the corner for whispers. I was finding out that a lot of whispering went on at Parramatta.

I had heard about Roger Rogerson. He was widely considered a very intelligent man, and at one stage he had been groomed as a future police commissioner. But that afternoon he obviously had other things on his mind, and he was another one who was definitely not happy to see me. "This is not the place for her," he told Ron. "You shouldn't have brought her here." Ron was clearly beginning to regret his decision now that he had lost face with the Dodger.

I gradually realised that the police at the table were wearing large gold rings. Theirs were similar: a chunky square with rows of diamonds. With a few drinks under their belts the boys would occasionally hold out a hand, fingers spread, admiring each other's rings.

With more alcohol being consumed, lips were loosening further. Despite this, Roger, Louis, the tall Chinese man and the two car salesmen remained cool. The only ones going berserk were the silly bloody detectives getting on the free grog. The sober men were there to talk business, not just celebrate and admire the gold rings. As the lunch went on, one of the detectives got so pissed he slipped off his chair and fell asleep under the table. This was amusing for a while, especially when he began snoring loudly. The entertainment was soon to change.

"What the fuck is that smell?" demanded Rogerson, his face turning rouge. The unfortunate bastard had soiled his pants. Even worse, he was wearing white jeans. As the stench wafted upward to those seated around the table, Rogerson went berserk. "Get that bastard out of here," he barked, getting to his feet. "Take him down and put him in the bloody car." Two of the boys I didn't know picked him up, one taking his arms, the other his legs. With strained expressions they carried him downstairs to the car park and left him unconscious in a police car. I never saw him again.

Eventually we were the only people in the restaurant. During lunch there had been a couple of other tables occupied by Asians. Knock-off time at 5pm came and went. We remained at the table talking, a favourite pastime of cops, trying to outdo each other with arrest stories.

As I was seated next to one of the used car salesmen, I borrowed his mobile to call home. "I'm doing lunch with the boys," I told my mother Irene. It was now a long way past midday. "I don't know what time I'll be home." If she had said anything I wouldn't have heard it anyway over the noise from the others at the table.

People had started arriving for dinner, but maybe only about two more tables were occupied by this time. Bayeh and Rogerson again moved to another table to play Chinese whispers. The Chinese man and the used car salesmen eventually left. As he favoured me with the occasional glare, Rogerson might have realised why I had left the Gaming Squad, that I had stood up against corruption and had not physically been safe there any more. Either that or he perceived that I wasn't like the others.

The cops stayed talking shit at the main table until they couldn't drink any more. When the bill came everyone looked nervously at each other. Who was to pay?

"I'll get that." Louis to the rescue. There was a sigh, then smiles all around. For a moment there ... Mind you, big lunches were pretty common for the Parramatta Detectives and rarely paid for. This one had been different, however. Some of the big players of the time had been present. Serious business was going on and I had entered dangerous territory.

Here I was sitting with a bunch of crooks who were wearing what I suspected was stolen jewellery. Just by being there I was afraid that I might be implicated in their activities. I was also frightened that if they found out I had supported the arrest of two cops at the Gaming Squad they might kill me because I might have too much information about them. I was being drawn into the dark circle of police connections with Sydney's underworld, and it was time for decisions.

How did I find myself here in such a short time? How did a girl from Glenorie, a farming community northwest of Sydney, a girl who could not read or write until she was nine years old, end up sitting with criminals?

All I had ever wanted to do was the right thing, although I was never exactly sure what that was. Maybe help people, hoping to do my small bit to make the world a better place. Spending all my life trying not to be like my deadbeat family, I dressed well and studied at university to try and better myself. Yet scum always seem to be able to tell where you come from. A pair of expensive shoes can't hide a childhood of deprivation and hard knocks. They thought I was one of them, and could be intimidated, easily manipulated within the detective clan. What they underestimated was my fighting spirit.

On the long drive home to Glenorie after lunch that day, I decided not to continue being swept along for the ride, being compromised by corrupt cops. Desperately trying to be accepted as one of the boys, I had never pretended to be an angel. Getting free drinks and meals was a basic requirement if you wanted to be a detective. But that was as far as I was prepared to go. I was unable to play on their terms – if that was going to be the cost of being a detective, it was too high.

This was one of the biggest decisions in my life and a turning point for the New South Wales Police Force. Phil Arantz had been locked in the nuthouse for making public that police were producing misleading crime statistics; Michael Drury had been shot, Kim Cook had been bashed. Now it was time for the first woman to stand up and fight the way business was being done.

CHAPTER 1

BECOMING A COP

When I was accepted for the Redfern Police Academy I was thrilled; when I walked through the gates for the first time I was nervous and excited. It was February 1984 and it had been a hot summer. I was a twenty-year-old size 10 with long blonde hair. It was scary how fit and healthy I was. I had run laps around the oval a million times and I was becoming a common sight running along the Old Northern Road at Glenorie. Never going to be this fit again, I had been training every day for three months to get here.

I had been working as a service station attendant, filling tanks and checking oil and tyres back in the days when service stations gave service. I was going out with my friend Maria's brother Mark whom I loved dearly, but he gave me an ultimatum. It was him or the Police Force; there was no way he was going out with a copper. He didn't realise there was no other choice for me. So we said goodbye.

The old buildings looked formidable. A three-metre fence of brick and steel circled the premises. Probably constructed around the turn of the twentieth century, the two-storey dark brick buildings had terracotta-tiled roofs. The mounted police section covered a large square block between Bourke and Baptist streets, with the stables on the ground floor and accommodation and offices above. The aroma of straw and horse manure was ever present. In the centre of the building was a large archway that gave access to Crown Street. The mounted police had begun and finished their patrols through these gates for at least a hundred years.

The Police Pipe Band and Military Band were upstairs in the building block near the gymnasium. We would hear the eerie sound of the pipers tuning up in the morning. This was a time when the bands would perform regular engagements at nursing homes and shopping centres, as well as on state occasions. They were a community service, and sometimes hearing one of the bands was the only contact some people had with the police, a positive one at that. It was a great public relations initiative. Then the name changed from Police Force to Police Service, and they took away the service.

When Ted Pickering became police minister he shut down the Police Pipe Band and the Police Choir. It was a sad day when that happened. The Pipe Band, which had existed for fifty years, was one of the premier Highland pipe bands in the country. Thank God we didn't lose the Mounties. You can't put a monetary value on some things. Our mounted police are the oldest continually serving mounted section in the world, which is something to be very proud of. Yet there was talk that they were too expensive. I wonder if these talkers have ever seen the Mounties work crowd control?

The buildings surrounded an expanse of hallowed turf known as the parade ground. Trainees were forbidden to walk on the parade ground, and only permitted to run across it during physical training. I soon learned that if you dared to sneak a short cut across it, one of the drill sergeants would scream at you. A tar-sealed roadway surrounded the grassed area, around which trainee officers spent many hours marching during drill practice. Marching in circles while being barked at by drill instructors, I came to appreciate, was an essential part of the police training curriculum. With time we all became proficient marchers, proudly strutting around with heads high, straight backs and arms swinging. Everything was extremely regimented and official.

After a fair bit of waiting around, my first day began with a short welcome speech by one of the instructors. Inspection time was next. As we stood to attention, one of the drill sergeants reviewed us, the troops. Some of the girls were told that their dresses were too short or their nail polish too bright. They were to be fixed by tomorrow. As for the guys, no matter how short their hair had been cut for the first day, they were told they had one week to get a shorter haircut. The old barber across the road was recommended to make sure they got the right style. The first week of each new intake must have helped the old bloke pay his bills.

When it was my turn to be given a physical examination by the old police medical officer (PMO), I was made to strip down to my bra and panties. Ordered to do pushups and some rather unusual balancing feats, I couldn't see what all this was supposed to prove. Some guys were complaining later that they had to do the old 'turn your head and cough' routine.

At the time my favourite forms of apparel were high stilettos, straight skirts and flattering tops. I had thick blonde hair and fair German features, and it didn't dawn on me until years later why the two female officers in the physical fitness section kept getting me to strip, take my measurements and test my body fat. I had very little in those days, but they were always poking and prodding me.

One of the recruits in my class proved to be an angel. He was Aboriginal and had worked in a cordial factory before coming to the academy; for the life of me I can't remember his name, only his smile. He helped me through the physical side of the academy training, staying back when we were going for runs of up to ten kilometres and pushing me across the line in time. With commonsense, heart and guts, he would have been a real asset to the Police Force. Yet he was eventually kicked out for poor spelling. It was a great loss. If he hadn't pushed me I would not have passed the physical training side of the course. I thank him for his kindness.

Women were required to pass the same physical fitness tests as men. I had to jump two-metre fences as well as run up and down Breakfast Hill. Located in Moore Park near the golf course, Breakfast Hill consists of a steep slope with a series of terraces. It was given its name by trainees as it was regularly adorned with the most important meal of the day, revisited.

When I joined, the men were generally white Anglo-Saxon males and at least 1.78m (5 feet 10 inches) tall. The handful of token females they allowed had to be more than 1.73m (5 feet 8 inches) in height. After completing their training, women were destined for school lecturing duties and taking statements from sexual assault victims. But that was only until they became engaged to be married, then it was 'out you go'.

Class 201, enrolled in the summer of 1984, was to be the second-last class to go through the Redfern Police Academy. We were told that the new breed of police would emerge out of Goulburn. The millions poured into the flashy new academy would be well spent; turning out highly educated officers. Times were a'changing. Not only women were going out onto the streets, but 'ethnics' and gays were also being welcomed into the ranks. Sadly, we were only welcomed in on paper. When it came to the real world, brutal and violent treatment was dished out to people of difference.

On the day of my passing out parade, my parents Irene and John were up early and getting ready just as I was returning from the party that had started the previous evening. Along with some of the guys from my class I had been drinking and playing cards as a pre-celebration. Twelve weeks of torture was nearly over. Young and excited, we looked to rosy futures in going to our new stations. I had been allocated North Sydney. This was a bloody long way from Glenorie, and the parking situation drove me mad from the minute I started there, but in those days the girlies mainly went to Central or Darlinghurst. North Sydney was much better, I was told. At Central there was a lot of cell work, and the Cross was sleazy. North Sydney area took in some of the northern beaches instead of the drabness of the inner city. It was also much quieter at night.

As I stood in my shiny spit-polished shoes I listened while all the speeches rolled by. Irene and John were so proud. They now had something positive to hold their heads up about. Standing to attention in my stiff new blue uniform, I too was feeling proud, even if the nausea caused by lack of sleep and too many gins and tonics was rising by the end of the ceremony. If swearing an oath on the Bible was taken very seriously, so was praying for the parade to finish.

There's a saying, "Scratch a copper and just under the surface you'll find a hero." We were all young and keen that day on the parade ground, yet it wasn't long before the spit polish lost its shine and the silver badge began to tarnish. We all wanted to make a difference as we joined. Maybe make the world a better place. Unfortunately, some were lost along the way, as they always are.

The academy was about hard work, lots of examinations and building physical fitness. After twelve weeks of intensive training at Redfern I was given a silver badge, a notebook and a Bible. I also received a Model 10 Smith and Wesson six-shot revolver, twelve shiny bullets and a set of handcuffs. Then, as newly attested probationary constables, we were all sent out to police stations to be set loose on the unsuspecting public.

CHAPTER 2

ALL IN THE FAMILY

They say the fruit doesn't fall far from the tree. But I disagree. I have always been the odd one out in my family. They would laugh when at the tender age of four years I would wring my hands and say, "Why me?" They thought it was funny. What I couldn't verbalise was, "Why was I born into this family?" Always hoping I had been adopted, I realised my dream of many years by obtaining my birth records from the hospital. I am probably the only person ever to be disappointed to discover they were part of their biological family.

To explain how my family ended up in such a sorry state I have to go back to World War I. My great-grandfather on my mother's side, Norm Passau, had been the mayor of Manly and very wealthy, even owning his own jewellery store. When Reginald, my grandfather, was born his mother died of tuberculosis a few days later. Everyone thought the infant wouldn't make it, yet anyone who knew Reg as an adult was not surprised he survived. Reg attended Scots College as a boarder at the tender age of three. He was a hard bastard, without empathy for anyone. The family blamed it on the fact he had not bonded with his family and never knew his mother, as well as going to boarding school at such a young age. Reg was short, only 1.68m (5 feet 6 inches), had beautiful blond hair all his life, and a bulbous nose. Apparently I have inherited his German looks.

When the war came, he was one of the first to sign up. He was very eager to go and do his duty, to travel overseas and kill people. Having the surname of Passau, a German town near the Austrian border, might also have made him keen to show his patriotism.

At the same time my other grandfather, James Webb, was enlisting. He was another pig of a man with a German background. Both my grandfathers sailed over to Gallipoli on the same ship, the HMS *Wondilla*. They never met each other but both of them were wounded, Reg losing the fingers of his left hand. Thanks to the war they both came back abusive, aggressive alcoholics. During the war other members of the family were interned in Australia because of their German background, but nobody ever talked about that. Dysfunctional alcoholic families have a lot of secrets.

Some returned soldiers were given land to farm on returning from war, and James became a soldier-settler in Leeton and Reg in Griffith. After marrying and having children, James moved to Glenorie on the northwestern outskirts of Sydney and bought an orange orchard. Reg, a hopeless gambler and alcoholic, lost his money and moved to

Galston near Glenorie, where he rented his farm. Again both men were neighbours.

Reg and his two sons worked for many years at Garden Island. "The docks are a tough place," Reg used to say when I was small. "Always get a government job." I didn't know what he meant at the age of four, but I sure do now.

Being blind by the time he received his medal for serving on Gallipoli, Reg could only feel it. He still had strands of blond hair when he died, but was for the most part bald. (Another characteristic of our lot.) He loved listening to the boxing on the television. Irene would let me have half an hour of Bugs Bunny and then we would switch back to his boxing. We spent many hours fighting over viewing rights to the old black-and-white television on the poultry farm.

Reg lived with us until he was admitted to Concord hospital, where he eventually died a chronic alcoholic. Once when he was in the DTs, I found him flopping around on the floor like a mermaid with both legs in one leg of his pyjamas. Many times he was freaked out by all the evil little gremlins dancing at the end of his bed and glaring at him. He always thought it was funny the next morning.

Irene and John, the two youngest children of Reg and James respectively, met by destiny. Irene was only sixteen, with a bellyful of arms and legs that became my brother, when in 1948 she was rushed into St Stephen's Church in Macquarie Street, Sydney, to be married. She only had one good dress to get married in and it was unfortunately black. She was very upset at being pregnant when she was married; it was a shame she carried all her life, and a real scandal at the time.

According to my grandmother's birth certificate, her mother, my great-grandmother, had been an unmarried mother back in the 1800s too. For repeating history, Irene was emotionally punished by her mother. For the rest of her life Irene was obsessed with beautiful white weddings. She started on my glory box when I was six, determined that her daughter was not going to repeat the family tradition.

I strongly believe that some people are born without a chance at happiness and fulfilment. My parents were like this. I never saw them ever really enjoying themselves. (Being pissed doesn't count.) Irene and John never allowed me to call them 'Mum' and 'Dad'. Possibly they thought they were being cool, as it was the 1970s after all. Or subconsciously they knew they were not fit to be parents. Their alcoholism had progressed a long way by the time I came along in 1964. I hardly knew my brother, who had married and gone from the family by the time I was three. We have never had a real conversation, and it's hard to believe that we have the same parents. I was brought up as an only child.

Irene had been very attractive in her day. She was 1.5m (5 feet 1 inch) tall, German, with blonde hair and a great figure when she was young. She would never allow herself to be seen in public unless her hair was lacquered – after she had removed the multicoloured plastic rollers – and wearing Woolworth's Starlet foundation and bright red lipstick. But the grog caused a rapid decline in her deportment. By the time I started school she was a physical wreck. She couldn't dress herself, and got around in rags and cheap, cracked vinyl slip-on shoes. Her attitude was that you wouldn't waste good drinking money on clothes, but ironically she seldom stepped out of the car, as she was ashamed of the way she presented. She ballooned out from a size 10 to a size 22.

All my parents' money went on grog and poker machines; spare funds were never wasted on superfluous items such as doctors' bills or medicine. Irene and John believed that if an animal got sick you didn't take it to the vet, you just put it down yourself.

That once young girl with so much pride self-destructed physically, emotionally and spiritually. In Irene's later years of drinking she would rarely leave the house. She reached the point where she was so fat and unfit she could not put her hands up over her head to put the rollers in, or to peroxide the dark roots of her hair. She had one true friend left in the world – George, a little bantam rooster. Besides alcoholism, Irene also had an eating disorder. She was the first bulimic I ever knew, probably before the word was even invented. Irene would stick her head out the lounge room window and start coughing. Old George would come hopping around the corner on one leg. He loved hot meals! Irene thought this was extremely humorous and the revolting business continued for about three years after every meal.

Inevitably, one day Irene found George stiff as a board under the branch of a tree. Heartbroken, she wrapped him in one of her old nylon nighties and buried him. There was a wake that night, with Irene and John getting sloshed over poor old irreplaceable George.

My father John had always worked hard. He was only 1.75m (5 feet 8 inches), not very handsome, with a big nose and a large mole on his chin. His hair was always worn in a crewcut. As a boy he had been a boarder at Canberra Grammar and he remained very proud of the fact. During one athletics carnival he was victorious in the hop, skip and jump, and had his name added to a school honour roll. In later years when he slipped into Korsakoff syndrome from alcoholic brain damage, he would repeat the tale of this achievement over and over again as he shuffled around and pissed himself. John's other unfortunate party trick was to throw up pissed and lose his false teeth. The next day we would go looking for them and be praying that they hadn't broken. By about the age of twelve I was expert at supergluing his teeth back together.

Throughout his life he tried to make his own wine. He would crush anything resembling fruit into an empty flagon and add methylated spirits to it. When I was young I believed that if you cut a triangle into a watermelon and poured a bottle of methylated spirits in, it would magically turn into watermelon wine.

Irene and John thought that the best decision they ever made was to have all their teeth pulled out when they were both twenty-two. (They forgot that afterwards they went to the pub to get drunk and John nearly bled to death.) About the time I turned seventeen, Irene suggested that I do the same as I would not have to worry about visiting the dentist, nor would I ever have another toothache. She was serious. She and John never cleaned their false teeth, although occasionally John would rinse his under a tap. I received my first toothbrush when a dentist visited our school when I was about eight years old. My baby teeth turned black before they fell out. You cannot imagine how much money I have spent on dentists in the past fifteen years.

John rarely wore anything but khaki bib-and-brace overalls. He did, however, own a suit, the old pin-striped one that he was married in. It was made from thick brown woollen material. The fly had rusted shut; on the rare occasions when my parents were invited to a wedding or funeral, John always managed to get blind drunk and to piss himself. When I was eighteen, I bought him a beautiful navy blue suit from Lowes at Castle Hill, of which he was very proud. It was the second of the only two suits he would own in his whole life. I don't know why, but he never threw the old brown one out. He was later buried in the blue one.

Irene's brother Ken was a very sad alcoholic also. All his life he had just wanted to be loved by someone, and he never was. At times he would attempt to entertain people in the hope that they would like him. Instead, they used him and took advantage of him.

I thought everyone lived like we did and just that no one talked about it. "This is the Australian way of life," Irene would explain. I thought the Australian way of life sucked.

My childhood consisted of people drinking, smoking and sitting around talking rubbish. I had few, if any, pleasant childhood memories. It's hard to raise a child when your life is unmanageable and you are always looking for the next drink. I remember one fight when Irene was arguing with one of the neighbours in the side paddock. After a time she ran back inside the house, slammed the back door shut and crouched down, her hands over her ears. Suddenly a bullet sliced through the back door, through Irene's hair, and came to rest in the old kitchen dresser against the wall. She squatted motionless for a few seconds until she noticed a puddle at her feet. Having regained composure she leapt up screaming and ran to the bedroom.

Irene was unimpressed, to say the least, when she discovered late in 1963 that she was pregnant again, this time after fifteen years of marriage. Always a bit on the dramatic side, on the way home from the doctor's office she kept opening the car door in an attempt to throw herself from the FX Holden. All she managed to do, however, was wreck one of her shoes on the gravel. John had two black eyes for the whole of her pregnancy. Their appearance around town was a source of amusement for the locals. Of great concern to her was how a new child would interfere with her drinking. But I couldn't help that.

Life on the poultry farm was very dark for the whole family. In the 1970s it was not uncommon for the Parramatta detectives to pay us a visit, Parramatta being the head station for the area. I now had family members who rode motorcycles during the period when the Finks Outlaw motorcycle gang crossed the Queensland border and engaged in a gang war with the Hell's Angels Sydney chapter. A family member who was involved in a number of suspicious deaths, including a person being put on a spit and barbequed, was also implicated in several pack rapes.

With this lot as relatives, you can imagine what our Christmas gatherings were like. One year we had two stabbings between lunch and dinner. Even today I still have a problem with the Christmas tree. Not wanting my kids to be affected by my emotional baggage, I work very hard at not giving them my childhood. However, I'm not a good enough actress to hide the effect the tree has on me, as I walk around it and avoid putting on the decorations. Every year I begged Irene not to make me put up the tree. Without fail at some stage before Christmas Eve she would throw the tree, decorations and all, into the rubbish bin, because her own childhood Christmases had been so awful. She also got very drunk and depressed. It never mattered how much she promised not to do it; after a few drinks, even with the best intentions, that dark familiar expression would descend upon her. There is nothing sadder for a child than to wake up on Christmas morning with no presents and a pine tree in the bin.

CHAPTER 3

NORTH SYDNEY POLICE STATION

I guess I was lucky to be sent to North Sydney instead of going to the inner-city stations as new women police officers usually were. A woman detective I was later to meet in the Fraud Squad, told me horror stories of her early days at Central when she was sent down to the cells with a bucket of hot water to clean up the blood after prisoners had been bashed.

North Sydney was different altogether. It was the head station of No. 6 Division, and being situated at 96 Pacific Highway it was fondly known as 'Number 96'. A lot of *stuff* went on, mainly because there were up to twenty women at the station, so the place was 'overrun with bloody front bums' as the male officers not so kindly called us women officers. There was much bonking behind the scenes as well as on duty. Quite a few police marriages resulted as a consequence of activities at No. 6 Division.

At about five every afternoon the place would go pretty quiet; North Sydney was a business and residential area. Though there was some fraud work, occasionally we got a good car accident, domestic or shoplifting case. No. 6 Division and the Chatswood Patrol further up the highway were unofficial rivals, sometimes with weird results. Late one Sunday night a poor old derelict died in a North Sydney park. He was found by the blokes in the paddy wagon who, enjoying a few beers in the early hours of the morning from the comfort of the front seat, didn't want the trouble of lengthy paperwork. Loading the deceased into the back of the wagon they drove him to the main park in Chatswood's patrol. Bugger me if we didn't find him back in No. 6 Division a few hours later.

Police stations are divided into two camps. The general duties police who wear a uniform are in the majority, and then there are the detectives. This small elite group who do not wear a uniform run their own race. They are called in by the uniform officers, supposedly to do the more complicated and protracted investigations. At North Sydney the detectives' office was situated in a building a few doors up from the station. No one knew what they were up to. They could come and go as they wished in their flash suits, with only the detective sergeant to answer to.

You don't apply to become a detective, you're invited. Out of 14,000 cops only about 2000 are allowed to wear plain clothes. And to be invited to become a detective, you need to stand out from the sea of blue uniforms. How do you do that? Certainly not by being a conscientious, non-drinking, honest hard worker. You must fit the mould of those already in the club. You need the personality of a detective to even get a look in – which is: be a 'good bloke', the sort who looks as if he can be trained.

Having a detective to put your name forward is very advantageous. However, this is not enough on its own. Next you must pass a trial period working in the office, be road tested, so to speak. Put in various situations to see how you stand up. These might be situations such as 'money in a freezer', when executing a search warrant. Finally, you are invited to 'sit' the Bull Ring, a panel consisting of senior detectives asking questions on the Crimes Act. After this they can piss you off if they feel you are unsuitable. To be given a go at getting into plain clothes and then not making the cut is the ultimate humiliation in the force. I say force, not service, as believe me it is a force – one to be reckoned with.

If you pass the Bull Ring, you become a plain clothes constable. You then work with the big boys in the detectives' office as a driver/typist. After completing the Potential Crime Investigators' Course, you attend detective training. If you pass that, you are awarded a framed certificate and the qualification of Designated Detective. You are now a fully fledged member. By then they really have you by the balls, which is unfortunate if you don't have any. Of course female detectives are never taken seriously anyway, even today. They rarely become senior partners on a team and their job is usually to make coffee, type and drive.

In the first six weeks at a police station probationary constables are allocated a buddy trainer. This poor bastard gets the same pimple-faced kid for every shift of their first six weeks at the station. Unfortunately, I spent most of my early days at

North Sydney with Senior Constable Dave 'Bowie' Bowden. Bowie was nearly two metres tall, with a sunken chest, short brown hair and a lot of acne scars, who lived on a diet of McDonalds. I was so short beside him that we must have looked ridiculous together, walking into jobs.

With all the bonking going on at North Sydney at the time, they gave Bowie female probationers only because he hated them so much. I guess the supervisors knew we would be safe physically, if not psychologically. In that first six weeks I nearly had a nervous breakdown.

Every time we drove into a new street I would be looking for the signpost. "What street are we in now?" he would bark about every ten minutes. If I didn't know the name of the street he would screech the car to a halt. "What if I was shot right now?" His face turned red. "How would you call for backup if you don't know what bloody street we're in?" I was in constant anticipation of a barrage of abuse. But if some assailant in North Sydney had shot him, I wouldn't have been able to call for help anyway; he never let me drive or use the radio.

Bowie would be yelling at me, talking to the police radio and trying to drive all at the same time. I was more likely to be killed in a car accident. Actually, we did have one in the rain one night; he skidded into an oncoming car. That was my fault, too. Or so I heard him say while 'bagging me' out to all the police at the station who would listen to him.

I attempted to warn all the girls who arrived at North Sydney after me to be careful and to just try and ride out the six weeks as best they could. The girl he had from the academy a few classes ahead of me was named Bridget. She was small and sexy with blonde hair and ample curves. (I still don't think she could have been the regulation height so I don't know how she got in.) She was really damaged by her six-week introduction to police life with Bowie. She was later kicked out of the cops when she burnt her own car with the assistance of her druggie boyfriend for the insurance money. Last time I saw her she was working in the toy department of a Target store.

On the evening of 28 July 1984 we were called to attend the Sydney Harbour Bridge because there was a man outside the safety fence. As we pulled up in the patrol car, we could see the guy standing on a workman's platform looking blankly out over the harbour. When we called out to him he just waved us away. We had a jumper. Bowie radioed for backup.

Before long, two lanes of the bridge were closed, with highway patrol cars and flashing lights galore, all there for a look. Cops will often travel long distances if there is a 'show' on or a good 'dead'un' to gawk at. The Cliff Rescue Unit was summoned and the supervising sergeant came down. All the police were standing around for what appeared to be ages, talking, no one knowing what to do.

Deciding to speak to the jumper I discovered that he too hated women. Apparently we were all sluts and, oh yeah, he was going to jump. He leaned out over the water a couple of times and I thought that was it. Then in a moment of clarity, he shuffled back slightly. "Can I have a cigarette?" Maybe it was a last request.

"I'll take it to him," I said, the eager trainee officer.

"No, you can't," insisted Bowie. "He hates women, remember?"

"Can I bring you a smoke?" I offered, cheerfully ignoring my buddy.

"Yes. Yes, I want you."

In the next instant I was being hoisted up over the barbed-wire safety fence. I stood out on the platform and talked with this guy smoking cigarettes. I have always hated smoking. It seemed like I was on that cold windblown platform for hours.

It turned out he had travelled down from the country with his best mate and his fiancée to get married the next day. They had pulled up on the side of the road to sleep and he had awoken to find his bride bumping uglies with his best mate. To try and humour him, I assured him this was normal. "All girls are sluts before they get married. They get scared and sleep around before making the big commitment."

We then smoked several more cigarettes, which I felt was more likely to kill me than being pushed from the bridge. I gained his confidence, I think, because we spoke the same language and both came from a farming background. The boys were in shock that a woman could do something that they couldn't; their plan was to wait and see whether he jumped or just got sick of being out there. The police have since discovered that women can be an asset in domestic disputes as they can often defuse volatile situations.

After I had convinced my new best friend to climb back over the safety fence and not hurl both of us into the inky darkness, he was taken back to North Sydney police station. He was shoved in a cell until Bowie and the station sergeant could figure out what to do with him. About half an hour had passed when I went to look through the hinged flap of the heavy metal cell door. The guy was hanging by the neck from a noose made with his belt. I screamed for help; it had been all too much for one night.

Bowie came running frantically with a set of cell keys. In all the panic, do you think he could find the key to open the cell door? It seemed to take forever. Finally the bolt shot across. Bowie ran in and wrapped his arms around the guy's legs, pulling them into his chest and lifted him up, taking the weight from around his neck like one of those punching bags down at the gym. More help was not far behind and the guy was cut down. Luckily he was only unconscious and was brought back around reasonably quickly.

Bowie could occasionally be compassionate and he had a big talk to this guy when he came to. After several cups of coffee he was allowed to sleep in the cell for the night. Bowie obviously felt sorry for him. Perhaps this was why he wasn't charged with trespass on the Harbour Bridge. Or maybe it's because he was a suicidal male placed in a cell, unsupervised and with his belt and shoelaces.

A few weeks later I was called into the inspector's office. He told me I would not be officially acknowledged for my actions on the bridge. The bloke hadn't jumped, and they didn't want to get the Cliff Rescue in trouble. In all the excitement they had sent me over the rail without a safety harness. "What if you had died?" explained the inspector, "What if he had pushed you over the edge? That wouldn't look good. Just let sleeping dogs lie." I had to think of the boys in Cliff Rescue, it seemed.

I walked out very confused, not understanding all the politics. I was to find out many years later that a small notation had been made about the incident on my service register. If I had been a boy, things might have been different. Maybe I'd be the hero I always imagined I could be in the force.

While working at North Sydney I celebrated my twenty-first birthday. The only other birthday party I'd had was my tenth. That had been a disaster, because the idea of having people at the house had stressed out Irene so badly that she went and had a heart attack the night before. After the doctor arrived it was decided to treat her at home as she refused to go to hospital. We had an old Indian doctor who allowed her to get her way. Irene could only be got into hospital with a whip and chair, and then it was mandatory to visit her every day with a couple of vodka and passionfruit UDL cans. She had an intense fear of doctors, coupled with the fact that she could not get a drink in hospital.

Another time she fell out of bed drunk onto her McWilliam's bottle of port, gashing her leg, which unfortunately abscessed below the hip. It eventually turned black and she was placed on a drip, but she refused to go to hospital. She must have been strong to survive. The old Indian doctor cut her leg open several times while she was in bed, and black, stale-smelling blood oozed from the wound. She was lucky not to contract blood poisoning and die, especially with our dog Shep under the bed scratching for fleas.

I had been a bit traumatised after my tenth birthday party from being told I was a greedy girl for wanting a party, and look what I had done to my mother. Apparently I was responsible for having nearly killed her. So I wasn't too keen about having a twenty-first party. It was, however, a cracker! The local electrician came the night before to string up party lights, as there were no external lights at the rear of the house. We had a huge crowd with a live rock band, and lamb on the spit. The dunny, being so far away, was a problem. But everyone seemed to cope or make do at least.

I will never forget that I bought $800 worth of grog for that party – it was a lot of money back then. At least we had a fully stocked bar. Aunty Doris, a binge alcoholic, was the most daring on the night. The young boys kept coming up to me complaining they had been grabbed on the you-know-what by a little old lady. I knew who the culprit was straight away. When sober she was so dignified, yet with alcohol added, watch out. Aunty Doris was the last one standing on the night, or should I say crawling. She came out of the bathroom naked on her hands and knees.

One of my Police Academy classmates was stationed at the Air Wing and couldn't make the bash. He managed to add to the spectacle by making a low-level flyover in the police chopper with all sirens and lights going.

An old sergeant told me when I was at North Sydney that if I wanted to get ahead in the job, I would have to go to university and study. The job was changing and the police were getting into education. Well, that was all I needed to hear. It was like: 'so where do I sign?'

I enrolled at Charles Sturt University in Bathurst to do an Associate Diploma in Criminal Justice (Police). When I started it was called Mitchell College. Twice a year I would travel up to Bathurst for residential lectures. Much of this time was spent in the Rafters bar. I also loved the cafeteria food. Even today, give me Woolworth's for lunch and I'm in heaven. I ate out only once when I was a kid, and that was at the Woolworth's cafeteria in Parramatta. It was such a treat I never got over it.

I had a couple of boyfriends at North Sydney, but my first real police romance was with a colleague named Brendan Short. He was tall, dark and simply beautiful to look at. It never bothered me when he sneaked glances at his own reflection as we walked past shop windows. I was young and smitten.

The first year was good, and we had lots of fun. However, after a while I noticed a few things. Brendan liked wearing my underpants under his police uniform. This seemed okay at first, but then it started to dawn on me that this had nothing to do with me. I would watch him working the old-fashioned switchboard, the one where you pull the plugs on cords out to shove them in a big board to link calls to the station. What would others think if they knew he had on bright pink knickers under his navy blue trousers?

Sex with Brendan was starting to get kinky as well. *He* wanted to play the girl part. Believe me, this is always a bad sign. The icing on the cake came when on a holiday in Fiji I walked in on him in the hotel bathroom. He was sitting down to piss. "Why do you do that?" I asked, looking confused.

"I'm a woman, trapped in a man's body."

It took me a while to process that one. Sure, he had always worn a lot of pink and lemon. And the tattoo on his chest was a picture of a seahorse. But this was a hard one to get around.

After our relationship ended I was broken-hearted for a long time. I tried to convince myself I didn't care that he was a girlie inside, or that he preferred sex with the vacuum cleaner. But I look back now and think, *Thank Christ I got away from that one.* Besides his predilection for anal sex with carrots from the vegetable crisper of the fridge, I couldn't stand his family. His parents had divorced when he was young and all the kids were affected. A lot of shame came from the fact that his parents had to get married, as his mother was pregnant with Brendan. He was so different from the rest of them, I used to think he must have been adopted too. For his sake I hope he was. My family was frightening, but they were up front. You got what you saw, but the families who bung it on and put up the fronts I find to be the really scary ones.

One day at North Sydney stays in my mind. It was an early start this particular morning, getting up at 5am to do the prison van run. Picked up at North Sydney by the tired old senior constable, I sat in the front seat all the way to Long Bay gaol. On arrival I walked into the main reception yard. The Bay is a horrible, imposing place. Inside, prisoners were carrying on a treat, especially the gays. They did not want to be touched or searched by a woman before they went into the back of the van.

The odd wolf whistle from the prisoners was embarrassing. It must have been a novelty to have a woman come into the gaol to search them. The men lined up behind the caged area. One by one they went into the back of the van. I then sat on a hard metal seat in a separate locked section at the very back. I get terribly carsick, and to be in an enclosed small section, going sideways, with no windows and little ventilation was worse than even the prisoners had to endure.

We began the long boring trip all over Sydney to each of the courts where the different prisoners were remanded to appear.

From the van they would be handed over to the police on court duty near a rear entry at each court. Boredom was etched in the faces of the court constables. Court process is a place to work if you don't have a career path. Sometimes guys are transferred there as a punishment – one reserved mostly for dickheads or non-drinkers.

We had visited three courts already and I was really starting to feel green. Unable to see where we were going, I was surprised when the van suddenly stopped. I opened the rear door and sunlight hurt my eyes. Squinting, I looked over six worried faces. Two of them belonged to detectives, the rest to uniforms. They ushered me away from the rear of the van, their guns drawn. I looked back confused; the driver, now at the rear of the van, looked stressed. We had returned to the courthouse we had left only minutes earlier. Swinging the door open, a detective dragged out a prisoner by the hair. After a few good punches to the ribs he pulled the prisoner through the open door to the courthouse. Screams were heard from inside. All the other police scrambled through the doorway, leaving me back at the van. Puzzled, I looked into the face of the driver.

"What was that all about?" I asked.

"It's your lucky day," he told me. "The bloke we dropped off last ratted on that piece of shit. He was charged with killing his wife and two other people. You were going to be next. He's got a replica gun down his pants. You mustn't have found it. He had pulled it out back at the District Court and was going to use it on you when we stopped again."

"What do you mean?"

"One of the prisoners took pity on you because you're only a kid and put him in. He told them he was going to get your gun on the next stop and shoot you in the head."

Having a small black gun pulled on me would have worked. He would have taken my gun off me with little trouble. I didn't realise how dangerous were the bastards we were moving around. These guys weren't going to court for having a bad haircut. What chance would a skinny young girl have against these desperados?

I didn't talk to prisoners as if they were garbage, as I had seen other police do. Treating the boys with dignity, I had still almost lost my life. A few of my family had been inmates at different times, so I saw things from a different angle to most. The compassion of that prisoner who saw me, and not the blue uniform, touched me. I don't know who he was, but I thank him.

The old senior sergeant at North Sydney was waiting for me when I returned to finish my shift at the station.

"Fuck me, you were lucky."

"Yeah. It's still dawning on me just how much."

"I can't understand why a crim would go out on a limb for a cop like that. You'd think he would have liked to see you done over. He's in for it when he gets back to the Bay."

I was never rostered for prison van security again. Soon I was given the opportunity of rotational experience at Kings Cross Drug Squad. I jumped at the chance. I didn't like the mundane duties of the blue uniform very much. There must be more challenging work, I thought, than filling in forms for car accidents and going to domestics.

CHAPTER 4

HAPPY DAYS ON THE FARM

On Sundays alcohol couldn't be purchased from the local pub unless you were a day traveller. This required the family going for a long drive to get grog from a pub outside the local area. We would drive all the way to somewhere like Wiseman's Ferry just so they could get a drink.

Why didn't they just buy extra on Saturday? Because they were alcoholics. If it was in the house, every drop would be consumed. Then the fights would start. I belonged to the generation of kids who spent their Sunday afternoons sitting in the back seat of old Holdens in hotel car parks while their parents got smashed inside. In the back of the ute, one glass of red soft drink and a packet of chicken chips were my companions. Busting to go to the toilet I sat there in all kinds of weather, waiting for them to finish. The old HR Holden was rolled a few times on trips back home. As it wasn't mandatory for cars to have seat belts when I was growing up, how I wasn't killed I'll never know.

There were horrific family fights on the poultry farm, too. Once John pushed Irene through a plate-glass door. Another time he stabbed her in the eye with a steak knife during dinner. Not long afterwards he found himself with a Wiltshire knife protruding from his chest. He was lucky it didn't puncture his lung or enter his heart. Poor old John was rushed to hospital on many occasions. He ended up looking like a patchwork quilt before he died. He always reckoned the closest Irene ever came to killing him was the time she caught him in the grain silo. Realising where he was hiding, Irene released the chute, letting all the chook pellets pour onto the ground. John was sucked down into the pellets remaining in the silo, nearly suffocating.

John got the better of Irene in a fight when they were young, but in latter years she returned the favour tenfold. One of her favourite tactics was to circle her left fist in front of his face to get his attention. While he was mesmerised by her left she would crack him with a full-blooded right cross. Why this worked every time was deeply mysterious.

In 1970 when I was six, grandfather James, John's father, died in his sleep. He was buried the following Monday. As I had no friends to stay with, Irene and John left me at the local paper shop to look at the cards on the stand until they returned from the funeral. It was pretty horrendous as they were gone for hours; the graveyard is near the James Ruse hotel. I can't imagine what the people at the shop thought I was doing there all that time. Imagine how I felt the following Friday when I was left there again so they could bury my grandmother. Alcoholic marriages are often like that. If one goes the other is unable to continue alone. Some call it dying from a broken heart, maybe it's what happens when you can't be co-dependent any longer. A few weeks later grandfather Reg decided to pack it in too. Back to the bloody paper shop.

We moved from the poultry farm into the old farmhouse at Glenorie that James had left my father. The property had been reduced from 109 acres down to an acre and a quarter. That's what happens when your grandfather is a gambling alcoholic. Most of the property was thrown away in dribs and drabs in card games and poker machines. This was sad enough, but worse than this, the place was haunted. I don't believe in ghosts but I've sensed an evil presence there. James had bought the place from a government official whose title was 'master of lunacy'. In earlier times if you were an alcoholic the master of lunacy would step in, sell all your possessions and lock you away in some lovely place like Callan Park asylum or Gladesville psychiatric hospital. Shock treatment and cutting the frontal lobe of your brain were the usual cures for insanity. Certainly my grandparents needed locking up by the time they died.

An old Russian guy had lived on the farm previously. He had a fully working still on the place when James bought it, and endless bottles of potato wine were hidden all over the place. It wasn't surprising he had also gone nuts on the grog, considering his legacy. The place seemed to have a grog monster curse on all those setting foot in it; everyone known to have lived there came to a sticky, alcoholic messy end. It was a wise decision to eventually sell the family home and get the hell out of Glenorie, leaving the phantoms behind.

At the age of ten I took over the running of the household. It began when Irene came to *me* with a red rates notice. "What are we going to do?" she pleaded. "They will sell the house up if we don't pay it." That week I started work on a neighbouring carnation farm after school and at weekends. The Sicilian family I worked for accepted me like a daughter, and was the first family I ever felt part of. Ross, the father, was kind and fair, paying me at the same rate as the adult workers, mainly because I worked just as hard as they did. Although I didn't know what it was back then, being a bit hyperactive was an asset to me – it meant I could get through more work in a day than some people could do in a week.

Ross's daughter Carmella and I became best friends. We would work twelve hours a day in the paddock while dreaming of the day we would marry and escape. We planned to have six children each. Carmella achieved that dream and has six of the most beautiful children I have ever seen, apart from my own of course. Hers was an arranged marriage, and she and her husband are the most happily married couple, working their own farm now in Glenorie. One of the most joyous experiences I have is to pay them a visit.

Carmella left school when she was twelve, only completing half of Year 7. "I don't speak the English," her father would explain whenever the Education Department came around. It worked. After about four visits they gave up and Carmella spent the next five years on the property. At her engagement party she met her future husband John for the first time, and ever since he has adored the ground she walks on. They are still in love after all these years; it seems that fairy tales do happen.

I always felt too fast for Glenorie while I was growing up. Ever since I was a little girl, Irene had told me I was going to be a policewoman. Unfortunately for both of us, she thought the job involved giving talks in schools and answering the phone. Irene imagined that having a copper in the family would add some respectability. Then there was the hit list of people she wanted to get. Irene preferred a fight to a feed and would often tell you so. If one day she got the shits with you, that was it. Even if she saw you in the street twenty years later, she would run up and yell in your face. No one could hold a grudge quite like old Irene. She was only small, but she had mad eyes that made big men back down.

School was a painful experience. Unable to spell my name until I was nine, I also found maths impossible. I was sent to a two-teacher primary school in the area, which was like a bush school. The lady who took the infants was very kind and understanding, and I loved her with all my heart. However, when I went into the other classroom I was to endure systematic cruelty. The male teacher, the headmaster at the time, was a bastard.

Classes were arranged in rows, third class, then fourth, fifth and sixth, with about six kids in each year. Because of my learning difficulties I was not allowed to sit with the other kids and was placed at a desk on the back stage at the rear of the classroom. I suffered four years of humiliation. When I wasn't on the stage I was often locked in a dark storeroom and was also caned on many occasions.

While this headmaster took a dislike to me, a cousin of mine was allowed to sit on his knee at the desk and do her schoolwork. Another poor kid spent most of his time at school out of the classroom mowing lawns. When I told Irene that the headmaster used to lock me in the storeroom, her helpful suggestion was that I should steal all the pencils and rulers I could get. I was also the only kid in the school *not* allowed to go to scripture lessons, which resulted in my standing outside the headmaster's door while any godlike stuff went on. Only allowed to attend church for weddings and funerals, I had no concept of a God or higher power. I believed I was all alone and that if I wanted something to happen I just had to put the effort in.

I'm sure I did drive the headmaster crazy with some bizarre behaviour. My warped sense of humour has often landed me in trouble. At the end of sixth class I stuck a potato up the exhaust pipe of his car and wrapped it in toilet paper. Thanks to that trick the primary school end-of-year party was cancelled. With time my sense of humour developed into the black variety, indispensable in the New South Wales police.

Galston high school was another challenging period of my development. The primary school headmaster thought I was retarded, so I was placed in Year 7E. But when I was eleven, the lights came on one day, and everything fell into place. All of a sudden I could read and comprehend concepts. By Year 10 I had advanced to the B class. I had been so poorly graded I went up a class in most subjects every year. (Except maths; I still can't do it!)

In high school there was an abused child named Maria who didn't function very well. The kids picked on her; kids can pick up these things and be very cruel. Even then I hated to see injustice and I went to her rescue. It would be to my detriment, as it just gave the bullies someone else to pick on. But I have always tried to help the underdog.

My main concern during my high school years was to make as much money as I could. I knew I didn't belong in my family or in the town. Being as hyperactive as I was enabled me to hold down at least two jobs. At high school I also worked on farms in my spare time. By the time I was fifteen I could afford my first cruise holiday, a trip on the *Oriana*. I didn't enjoy it much, though, as I was too young and a bit lost.

Years later and after more saving I took my kids, which is what I considered Irene and John, on a couple of cruises. It was sad that during their last cruise, just before they died, my parents refused to leave their cabin. A bloke down the hall was selling them litre bottles of rum for $10 each. Irene would watch the porthole in the cabin, which she would pretend was a washing machine, as she lay in bed sipping her rum. She hated rum, but it was far too much effort to go up to the bar. I had to get the doctor to come up from the surgery in the bowels of the ship to dress the weepy ulcers on John's legs. He was very bloody angry at being so put out. "Why would you take alcoholics on a cruise?" he asked with a glare.

It was a very good question. For years, since the time I acquired my driver's licence, I would take my parents on scenic drives in the car, hoping to give them some joy. It never worked. A bottle always accompanied them so they could drink in the car. They couldn't have cared less where I took them as long as they were drinking. It was like hitting my head against a brick wall. But they were my naughty children and I loved them, I suppose.

Keeping my head down, I worked hard and finished my HSC, the first person in my family to do so. I continued working on farms, in bars and the local service station until I was old enough to join the cops. It was all I ever imagined doing. I applied in 1983, as soon as I turned nineteen. There was never a question concerning what I was going to do with my life. I just wanted to be a good cop, do my job, help people and make a difference.

CHAPTER 5

KINGS CROSS DRUG SQUAD

My first experience in plain clothes investigations was at the Kings Cross Drug Squad, between 3 November 1985 and 2 February 1986. This was certainly a learning experience. It was nothing but a rat's nest. Our office was in the basement of Kings Cross police station. It was a small, underground concrete bunker with no natural light and the musty smell of damp carpet. Cardboard boxes filled with paperwork were piled up in corners. One of the sergeants was obese and ill-tempered. Long black hairs protruded from his ears and red-veined nose and his John Lennon-type reading glasses only made his already large head look even bigger.

On my way to work early, I would walk up the main strip, Darlinghurst Road, to the police station. The working girls on the footpath would tell me, "I've already paid sergeant so-and-so today." Sure enough, the roster confirmed every time that the bloke they had mentioned had started at seven that morning.

I was only to be at the Cross for three months, and that was more than sufficient for me. The older members of the squad would refer to the new investigators as 'woodchucks', young officers on rotation from their usual station to gain some surveillance experience. I went there after being told it would look good on my service register. The old seasoned detectives in the office were shady and colourful characters. They had a habit of whispering and talking from the sides of their mouths. All the young investigators were treated like scum, the shit on the soles of their shoes.

I spent hours walking up and down the main strip of the Cross. I loved the excitement of the night, but the picture was different in the light of day. The early mornings were the most disturbing. Young girls bombed out of their scones leaned against grubby walls, slowly becoming aware the sun was rising. These early morning visions always made me feel a bit sad as I wondered what events had led such young lives to this place. Hoping to catch one more bloke before the night was over, some of the workers looked as if they were barely managing to hold themselves upright.

Betty and Chantal were streetwalkers I really liked because they had character. They were not pretty young things who had lost their way and who had a terrible drug habit to maintain. These girls were true professionals, real working girls who didn't touch drugs. Both had fluffy teased-up hair, and wore lots of makeup and very tight sexy clothing in satin or lycra. They looked like prostitutes in old 1960s movies. On my strolls up the strip I would usually stop and have a chat, often coming across them working outside the Pink Pussy Cat or Porky's.

Standing on the footpath for what seemed like hours, they propositioned the boys as they walked by. "You're too nice to be a cop, Deb," said Chantal one day. "You speak to us like we're humans, not like the other bastards. They speak down to us and usually only when they want a free favour. When you're been in this job as long as I have you see a lot of pigs come and go. Be careful of the blokes you are working with, they are not nice."

Chantal told me about her three children who were in private boarding schools in Melbourne. She was very proud of them and showed me photographs. The kids did not know that she flew up to Sydney to make quick money to give them a good education. In her day she would have been a real beauty, with a perfect curvy body, big boobs, long legs, thick red hair and green eyes. Chantal would have been pushing forty, which seemed ancient to me at the ripe old age of twenty-one.

On walkabouts I was also befriended by a short little hunched-over bloke affectionately known as Grimy Graham. I only ever saw him in brown cord trousers with matching jacket. This was summer, yet he was always covered up. Long, black greasy hair covered most of his pockmarked angular face, and his large nose jutted out below his slitted, darting eyes.

One day he slipped up behind me as I was coming back from my favourite haunt, McDonalds. "Do you want to get on?" were the first words he ever said to me.

"Yeah," I said, taken by surprise.

He laughed loudly. "I know you're a new copper, I've seen you walking up and down with the boys. I'm Graham. What's your name?"

"Debbie." He was cheeky, and I liked that. It seemed the only friendly people around were those who lived off the street. The cops were cold and stand-offish. They were too busy being big-city detectives.

The boys knew Grimy Graham very well. He was on the strip every day to get his heroin supply. He came from a very well-known wealthy family who had disowned him because he had AIDS. Graham had grown up with privilege, yet addiction had left him dirty and homeless, looking for his next hit. I felt pity for him, the boys saw him as a joke.

The detectives often took me to a strip club in Kellett Street. The décor was very 1970s, with an enormous birdcage suspended from the ceiling to accommodate exotic dancers. It was operated by a large Greek boy who called himself Stevie Stardust. Stevie was a local identity with his fat stomach and hairy chest covered in gold chains. His head was clean-shaven and he habitually wore sunglasses at night. He was an imposing figure; and I found him to be more of a gentleman than the blokes I was working with. One night under the mirror ball he told me he had been very badly done over by a detective who had earned his nickname of 'Greasy' partly because of his sexual habits, and partly because of the condition of his hair. He always gave me the creeps. I tried to get Stevie to explain further about his problems with Greasy, but he was too frightened. "Get out of here while the going is good, Deb," he would tell me. "This is no place for a young girl like you, you no belong here." It was good fatherly advice.

I hated the morning shifts, where we walked around stamping on syringes in the gutters. We would break them so the kids wouldn't use them on their way to school. AIDS was becoming a big deal back then, and everybody knew about it. "It's just a load of bullshit," the old sergeant would say. "It'll blow over in time. Either that or it will kill all the poofters."

One morning during coffee at a local cafe one of the pretty young prostitutes, no more than seventeen years old, told me she had AIDS. The fear and hopelessness were evident in her eyes. "You shouldn't be working the streets now, love," I told her.

"I promise to be careful," she assured me. "I always tell them. Most of them use condoms to be safe."

The ignorance of this deadly disease was shocking back then. Sadly, people are getting bored with it these days or maybe it is just a part of life; there is certainly not the fear and concern about it that there once was.

I don't know if it was the sex-charged environment or something in the water, but during my time at the Cross two different woodchucks pulled their penises out to show me while we were on walkabout. Not knowing how to react when this happened, I would think of clever responses afterwards. Maybe a comment concerning size would have been appropriate; however, the first dick flashed at me was actually huge. On the second occasion the idiot ran back to the office and told everyone I had had sex with him. All this hero did was to wave his dick in my general direction. He had a girlfriend at the time too. As I was young, my defence was to ignore his bragging bullshit, but that was a big mistake. I should have punched him in the face in front of everyone. He had me labelled as a slut among the other woodchucks. I would deal with him very differently these days.

Women police were still such a novelty that the boys didn't know how to behave, especially with a few drinks in them. Some had such big egos that they thought they were God's gift to women. How could we knock them back unless we were lesos? Not letting truth get in the way of a good story, I have heard about many amazing occasions when women in those uncomfortable culottes are supposed to have attacked men at work. My favourite story is the reason given around the station for a police car accident – that the policewoman was giving a head job at the time. It couldn't just be that the bloke was a lousy driver, of course.

On evening shifts we woodchucks would walk around in groups of two or three and look for wherever badness was happening. I think some of these kids had never seen marijuana before. Incredibly, they could walk around all day with their heads up their bums, looking trendy in the latest designer jeans, and not recognise a druggie when they fell over one. On the other hand, my family background and the fact that I had worked as a barmaid helped me pick a smackie at one hundred paces. Nearly every day in the first couple of weeks I would want to drag one or two back to the lockup to be charged. I was told to slow down as my enthusiasm was not appreciated by the charge room staff, who thought they already had enough work to do. "Picking up users on the street or smalltime dealers is not what the Drug Squad is about," one of my colleagues said through gritted teeth. I wondered why we were there then. All we did was walk bloody miles and do a lot of drinking. I was bored.

On the way out of the muster room one Friday afternoon I was cornered by the station sergeant. "You had better be careful," he warned. "You will be judged around here by the people you associate with."

"What do you mean?"

"Keep away from the bikies. They're all arseholes."

"Yeah, okay. Thanks for the tip."

The previous day I had been walking the strip with another sergeant and a woodchuck when I got into a long conversation with a bikie. The boys always parked their bikes on the strip outside the tattoo parlour and the sergeant was not amused. Unfortunately Hairy Mick was my cousin.

I continued to make small arrests on a fairly regular basis. I needed to fill in time, the shifts seemed so long when you had nothing to do. It must have been some genius's brainstorm to rotate one young police officer from each of the regions to give them plain clothes experience. Unfortunately, the regular detectives at the Cross found that we cramped their style.

I would fall over Grimy Graham and Chantal most days and would always get a smile and a kind word from them. Graham would sometimes give me tipoffs about druggies he did not like. "Why would he tell you that?" said the sergeant one day, filled with suspicion. He could not understand how a woodchuck could cultivate an informant in such a short time. All I had done was speak to Graham like a human being.

One day I was in the office on my own, finishing a column of paperwork. The rest of the office was up at the Bourbon and Beefsteak where, between four and five in the afternoon, the management would put on a hot platter of seafood for the cops along with a few free drinks. My train of thought was interrupted by the phone. "There's a sheila in the foyer who wants to see one of the detectives," said one of the uniforms at the inquiry counter.

When I walked upstairs I saw the young woman, blonde hair hanging down straight, wearing blue jeans and T-shirt, and with a big gap between her front teeth. Having briefly spoken to her a few times on street patrols, I knew who she was. "Can I help you?" I asked. "Everyone else is out."

"I don't want to talk to you," she said. "You're just a woodchuck."

I was surprised she knew the nickname the detectives had for us and I felt embarrassed. She appeared agitated and distressed. She looked around, fidgeting, "I'm going, you can't help me."

The following day Sallie Anne Huckstepp was found floating face down in a pond in Centennial Park. I was stunned. What hadn't she told me the previous day? Had she been able to speak to someone she could trust? Obviously not. I later heard that she had been given a speedball that would have killed a horse. Word had it that Sallie Anne had such a high tolerance to drugs that she had then been held under the water and drowned in the end. She had spoken out about a police conspiracy after the death of her boyfriend Warren Lanfranchi. In June 1981 Lanfranchi had been shot dead by Detective Sergeant Roger Rogerson in Chippendale's Dangar Place. Sallie Anne had blown the whistle in the media, insisting that police had murdered her boyfriend.

Before the end of my secondment to Kings Cross I was told by one of the other woodchucks that the Gaming Squad was a good place to work. I was still nursing a broken heart over

Brendan and was not keen to return to North Sydney. Besides, I was starting to consider what direction my career should take, and could not pass up an opportunity of working plain clothes duty, and so I applied. I had absolutely no idea what to expect.

CHAPTER 6

EARLY DAYS IN THE GAMING SQUAD

The Gaming Squad was only a short drive across town on the twelfth floor of the Remington building opposite Hyde Park. Many of the floors in the building were leased by the Police Department and housed other squads, including Homicide and Vice. When it was my turn to be interviewed, I was pointed in the direction of one of the glass-partitioned rooms at the rear of the large open-plan office. A couple of the more senior officers in their late fifties were seated behind a desk with a notepad and a few files in front of them. The usual questions and answers about my abilities and previous experience bounced back and forth. "Why don't you think about going to Highway Patrol?" suggested one of them. "They're starting to let women in there."

"I've never thought about going there. I want to be a detective."

"You have to think of the environment you'll be going into. I don't know if the Gamers is the place for a woman."

"Why not?"

"You would be the only female in a squad of hard-working, hard-playing blokes. The language around here gets pretty rough."

Driving fast cars sounded like fun, and being the first woman on a motorbike had its appeal, but I knew a real career path was in plain clothes. This was not an opportunity to let slip by. "Well, I'm used to hard work and I've been known to play hard too. A bit of swearing isn't going to bother me."

"Thanks for coming in, love. We'll let you know."

It's not what you know, it's who you know that matters most in the cops. One of the woodchucks I was working with at the Kings Cross Drug Unit was the Gaming commander's son, who put in a good word for me.

I started on what was referred to as 'the floor' of the Gamers on 9 March 1986. The desks were arranged for teams of four to six investigators. There were about sixty men and myself, the only bloody girl. There had been another, Claudia Campanelli, a young Italian girl who had left only days before I arrived after receiving a hard time from the boys. Or so I was told. Apparently she was too much of a nice girl and was easy game at night when the boys got on the drink. The guys made disgusting comments about her being Italian and what they would like to do with her. No wonder she ran. I began to wonder what I had walked into. They *were* rough-looking boys.

Our duties included attending at least three pubs on a race day, sitting, drinking and looking for SP bookies. On Wednesdays and Saturdays we were given $10 tax-free money from the 'slush' fund. The procedure required queuing in front of the sergeant's desk, marking your name off and being handed your cash. It was a great job if you were an alcoholic. Gamers were usually given a little sporty unmarked car to go with the drinking money when they did the rounds of the pubs. Yee ha! Going to work was more fun than a day off for most of the boys. Funny thing, though, the whole time I was at the Gamers, I don't remember many arrests of SP bookies.

Brian Ritchie, the sergeant who ran the team I was on, was known as 'Ritcho' to all the boys on the floor. Into body building, he was built like a brick wall, and competed in competitions and travelled great distances for his sport. He wasn't the only sporty cop around: the Police Force had its fair share of current and former rugby league players, and even a few referees, like Detective Sergeant Kevin Roberts. The force organised their shifts so work did not interfere with training and match days. They could always arrange their leave if they had to go on tour. They were big, dumb and built like brick shithouses but treated like heroes: useful attributes for boys in blue in those days. The other two blokes on my team were fat and middle-aged with long hair and needing a good tub.

At first Ritcho took me under his wing in a fatherly manner to show me the ropes. Not having the first clue about gaming, all I knew were poker machines because of my mother, who managed to put a small fortune into her favourite pokies at the Dural Country Club every week. "I've donated the money for the club's new extensions," she would say proudly.

One afternoon a sergeant stormed through the door. Almost foaming at the mouth he pushed over the chair next to me for dramatic effect. "Look here," he said to one of my colleagues. "I'm sick of every time I go near any bloody slopes they start yelling, 'You can't touch us!' The whole of Chinatown's in your bloody pocket!"

Ritcho calmly rose to his feet and took the guy by the shoulder. They walked to a corner of the office to have a serious conversation, which appeared to calm the sergeant down.

I was certainly spending many hours in and around Dixon Street. On those days dinner meant Chinese food. The restaurant normally chosen operated a big game upstairs. The waiter would bring out a huge live lobster on a wooden tray for our approval, then after a few moments he'd be back with it cut up at the table. The first time it happened my eyes nearly popped out of my head. It must have only been waved over a pot of boiling water, the bloody thing was still alive. We spent a lot of time talking to Asians while large games were going. A rule that operated at the time stated no more than eight people could be in the room while a game was on. The rooms in Chinatown were packed shoulder to shoulder. I looked on in wonder as old ladies played with $200 chips.

After dinner one night we headed back to the car. "I'm just going home for a minute," explained Ritcho starting the vehicle. "I need to pick up something." It only took about ten minutes to get to his home. In the driveway was a silver Mercedes with deep circular scratches on the bonnet and roof.

"Jesus, what happened here?" I asked.

"There's nothing like a woman scorned," he said.

"Your wife did this?"

"Not exactly."

Once inside, I waited in the lounge room while he took off to get whatever he had come home for. The photograph on the mantelpiece looked like his kids. They were older than I was. Ritcho came back into the room with a couple of glasses. "Gin and tonic is your favourite, right?"

"Yeah, okay."

"Here are some shots of the family," he said handing me a large photo album. "They've all grown up and left home. I've got this big house with no one to share it with."

I sat down on the lounge placing the album on the coffee table and began flicking the pages. Ritcho sat beside me on the arm of the chair. Feeling his hot breath on the back of my neck, I jumped up from the lounge. "Hadn't we better get back on the road?"

He got up without a word, grabbing the keys and headed back out the door. Feeling that I needed to explain why I wasn't interested, I told him about the complications in my life, having to care for two difficult parents.

About a week later I arrived at work with my usual takeaway cappuccino from the shop downstairs to find two suits at my desk. One was standing, the other looking through my duty book. "Can I help you guys?"

The one sitting at my desk identified himself as an officer from the Internal Affairs branch. "We're interviewing everyone in the office involved in the raid at Marrickville last week," he said.

On the two-minute walk across the park back to their office in Headquarters I racked my brain. It was my first time at Internal Affairs. Apparently a complaint had been made that police had stolen money, gold rings and a bracelet when they tipped over some old Greek men playing cards. My statement was typed for me by a smooth-faced detective constable while the officer dictated. It said I had seen nothing and no complaint had been made to me by the Greeks while I was searching the premises. This was basically true. It had been very noisy on the raid and I had been mainly out at the car, being the girlie. If anything had happened, I wouldn't have known. But I didn't feel comfortable that they were telling me what to say without even discussing it with me.

"Just sign here," said the officer, pushing the statement towards me across the desk. "You'll hear no more of this matter. This is just a formality." Having had no previous experiences with Internal Affairs, I thought this must be how things were done.

One Saturday afternoon we hit the office of an old Greek SP bookie who was in the last stages of dying from cancer. He wasn't a bad old bloke. Flanking him, we walked him out of the house and placed him in the rear of the police car. As I drove off, a silver-haired male in a navy suit ran at the car, yelling something. Thinking it must be the prisoner's bouncer I tried for the brake, but hit the accelerator instead. The car lurched forward with the guy sliding up the bonnet, his face coming to rest against the windscreen. "It's Chris Murphy!" gasped Ritcho. "You can't run over Chris Murphy!"

"Who the fuck's Chris Murphy?" I asked. Having rolled to his left, he was now on his feet standing beside the driver's door. "You all right?" I asked.

"Yeah, fine. I just rolled with it." Murphy brushed his sleeve.

"This man is my client and I need to speak to him immediately."

"Well, that's fine. You can speak to him after we get back to the station."

"Don't say anything, Angelo, until I get down to the station," he called out as we drove off. During the drive to the lockup Ritcho filled me in on Chris Murphy, a well known and well connected Sydney solicitor. Over the next ten years Mr Murphy became known as one of the most dynamic and sought-after criminal defence lawyers. He was a colourful character who, at one stage, had 'VERBAL' as the numberplate of one of his cars. He was one of the few criminal defence solicitors who really gave the police a run for their money when they were being cross-examined, because he had an intimate knowledge of how the police operated. Although he appeared to hate the police and their methods, many detectives respected his ability and determination.

Working on the floor of the Gamers was enjoyable most of the time. There was a lot of drinking, and as the only woman I did get the hard word put on me a fair bit. Ritcho was pretty determined, but I just wasn't interested. While he had good connections with the Asians, other teams seemed to have rapport with the Lebanese or the Greeks, and so on. It was as if certain sergeants had their territories marked out.

Getting really pissed one night, Ritcho went back to the office and pulled a supply of large firecrackers out of his locker. As I drove around Sydney to places where card games were happening, Ritcho would light a big one and throw it through the open door. They must have all hit the floor as the crackers went off. We would then drive off in the police car to the next victim for a laugh.

Not long after this Ritcho started to get all serious with me. "Our age difference is not that great. I really care about you. I have enough money to keep you happy." He just wouldn't take 'no' for an answer. When he pushed me against the wall of an elevator trying to kiss me as we were coming up from the basement to the office, I decided I'd had enough. Fighting him off until the doors opened, I ran straight into the ladies' toilet to get away from him. Mandy Price from the Surveillance Unit was putting her makeup on.

"What's wrong, Deb?" she asked.

"I'm sick of fighting these bastards off. Can't they get it that I'm just not interested?"

"They're all dumb pricks. Look, I'll have a talk to Rowan and see if we can get you on the Surveillance Unit. I had to go there because the same shit was happening to me. The floor is like a zoo. Full of animals."

Within a few days the boss of the Surveillance Unit, Detective Sergeant Rowan Hutton, came over to my desk. "You'll be working with us from now on. Grab your stuff," he told me.

Glad as I was to get away from the drunks, I knew nothing about surveillance, although I was eager to learn. The first bonus of the move was a shiny new sports car, mine to use as a member of the team. There was also a lot of cash around. We would let it build up, then collect a big payout every now and then. We worked from home, which meant we would start and finish in the field. At the start of the shift we would meet at a coffee shop or McDonalds near the target for the day. At the end of the day we just knocked off from wherever we had ended up and drove straight home.

The Surveillance Unit was shrouded in mystery; no one knew what we did. We were rarely seen, as there was no need to come into the office. The overtime also seemed unlimited and soon I had twenty-nine days of leave in the back of my duty book. I ended up going for a trip to the Northern Territory just to use them up. There was definitely a party atmosphere about the team.

I soon got to know the others. The other girl in the unit, Mandy Price, was a tall, skinny brunette with shoulder-length hair who looked as if a good gust of wind would blow her over. She had a heart of gold. Lucas Parker was a fat little bloke who seemed too short to get into the cops. He loved his tight leather pants and gold chains. He constantly played Wagnerian operas over the police radio back channel which we used to communicate between cars. We had scramblers so no one could listen to our operations. Lucas thought he was a turn-on for the girls, and no one had the guts to remind him about the bald spot on the back of his head. His imitation satin shirts were always undone much lower than they should have been.

By contrast, the boss Rowan Hutton was an old-school detective who was very good at his job, was softly spoken and always smartly dressed. Unfortunately, he had a limp from an old skiing accident which made him stand out when we were trying to follow someone on foot. We all wasted much of the time in beachside cafes and Paddington pubs, talking war stories.

One day, just back from holidays, Lucas picked me up from home on the way to the office, driving his own car. He was wearing a Hawaiian shirt and driving a bright yellow Torana and he looked ridiculous. But when he pulled into Pennant Hills police station, went up to the bowser and took a petrol docket book out of his glove box, I stopped laughing. "What are you doing? Are you mad?"

"Yes. I am mad. But I do this all the time. I couldn't be bothered syphoning the petrol out of the police car. You won't catch me sucking on a hose."

I just put my head down. "We're in for it now," I mumbled as a young constable came out as he was filling the car.

"Gee, you guys have good undercover cars," said the young cop. "I want to go there one day."

"Yes, it's a good life," smiled Lucas.

My first investigative job with the Surveillance Unit involved travelling up to Queensland for two weeks, looking for an SP bookie. Two Telecom boys travelled with us to make the job look legitimate. I had to share a hotel room with Rowan, my boss, because another married sergeant from the floor had his girlfriend with him, and they were given what was to be my room. They kept calling it the 'honeymoon suite', and I never saw them come out of it. Luckily the boss was a real gentleman so I had no problems with him. He was, however, nervous that his wife would find out he had shared a room with a woman.

The trip was based on the belief that the boys deserved a little break. Not knowing how things were done, I just went along for the ride. I didn't feel easy about it, but I felt out of my league, and I was having a lot of fun. Looking back now, if I had said anything I would probably have been thrown into uniform and prison escort duties if I was lucky.

During the time I was at the Gamers very little police work was done on the floor, or by the Surveillance Unit for that matter. There would be days when some officers wouldn't turn up at all and other days when we might only work for two hours. Some days people would turn up for work, have lunch at the pub or a cafe and then go home. It was not very productive most of the time. But it was all a learning experience for me.

On the way to an investigation down south for nine days with the Licensed Gamers, I stopped off at Cronulla to check on Uncle Ken, Irene's brother and a hopeless alcoholic whom no one else in the world cared about. He had bought a little one-bedroom unit near Cronulla beach with his payout from being a crane driver at Garden Island. His job involved a lot of eating and sleeping; they had to wake him up when they needed something moved. Fortunately, my grandfather had also worked there and managed to get Uncle Mick a job there too. Mick was shithouse cunning and lazy. He was, naturally, the union delegate and would look out for Ken.

You could actually see the ocean through Ken's bathroom window if you stood on your tiptoes. Unfortunately the smell of the small room in no way resembled the seaside. It was more like the men's dunnies at a notorious disco at Parramatta, where your feet stuck to the floor. Ken was lying in bed with a once-white sheet up to his neck. I could see where blood had been pouring from his partly open mouth. "I had some teeth pulled earlier today," he explained. The despondent, finished look in his eyes when I left told me that he was pretty crook this time. I still don't know why I left him there. Maybe it was because I was running late to meet the troops down south, or just sick and tired of getting bloody alcoholic relatives to hospital. Besides, drunks seem to hang on forever and just kill everyone else around them. I knew I would never see him alive again, but he wouldn't let me call an ambulance. He just wanted to be in his flat that he loved so much.

I'm not sure how I knew Ken was going to die. I believe my mother had the sixth sense, and so did her Aunty Margo. I think I've had a touch of it since my childhood, and it has helped me avoid some sticky situations. I sometimes sense when I'm going to hear from someone I haven't heard from for a long time by mail or telephone. I also feel the presence of people I know before I see them in crowds or shopping centres.

When I arrived at the pub where we had arranged to meet, the team was already on the way to getting pissed. Mandy had been into the port and the two boys, Pete and Mike, were really under the weather.

"Hi," I could tell things weren't as they should have been. "What's going on?" "Can't talk here," Pete replied sheepishly. "We'll tell you later."

Next morning I was told over Vegemite on cold toast that Mike had arrived the night before and proceeded to get *really* pissed at the club we were working on. The RSL club was targeted because some bastard was stealing coins out of the poker machines at night.

While on the drink a huge fight erupted, over the Parramatta Eels of all things, and Mike king hit the main suspect at the club. Unfortunately a posse of locals chased him down the road trying to, as they kindly put it, "bash the shit out of him". Thus the whole job was blown. We couldn't exactly return to Sydney and say to the officer in charge, "Got pissed and king hit the suspect," so now we had eight days to kill.

During this week Mandy was in a depressed state. She bought a fishing line and sat by the riverbank with a bottle of port. The boys put their heads together and made up bullshit surveillance logs for each day. If Mike had shown his head near the club he would have been lynched. Mandy and I were pretending to be Mike and Pete's girlfriends, there just to hang off their arms while they were conducting surveillance at the club. The senior cops organising the job thought we were only there to look good but not really be part of the investigation, so we were treated like dirt. The guys decided that because we were out-of-towners and girls we couldn't even go into the club on our own without them. Their opinion was that you needed a penis to do *real* police work.

When the long nine days were up, I decided to call in on Uncle Ken on the way home. I met Lucas at Mandy's place, which was a dingy little unit only a few blocks away, as he was just about to start another bodgy overtime shift and needed Mandy's car. He was going to spend the majority of his shift working as a DJ at a nightclub in Parramatta. I was going there for a drink, maybe even a dance, before making my way home. "Follow me and wait in the car while I just check on Uncle Ken," I told Lucas.

I knocked on the door. No answer. I made my way around to the verandah door, which was always unlocked. Everything was in complete darkness. I knew to shuffle past the greasy glass coffee table, always covered in beer cans and overflowing ashtrays. I missed the red velvet lounge, which was his pride and joy, and turned the light switch on. There turned out to be a reason why the stench was worse than usual. There was Uncle Ken on the lounge in the raw holding his old fella, dead as a doornail.

The room appeared to swim as I negotiated my way back to the balcony. I began screaming to the street below, but Lucas had the windows up in the shiny silver sports car and the music blaring, getting into the mood for his real work as a DJ. Finally, a guy walking along the street knocked on the car window because of all my yelling and Lucas waddled upstairs in his black leather pants. (Another of his many nicknames was Leatherman.) We met on the stairs.

"Ken's dead," I informed him.

"Bullshit."

As though I wouldn't recognise a naked dead bloke who had been rotting in the sun for nine days.

Upon reaching the door Lucas was introduced to death's aroma. "Yep, he's dead all right."

I was hysterical; there was no calming me down. Of course I blamed myself for his death, as did the family later. I had known he would soon be dead, his time had been up for ages. He was a dead man walking, a very lonely and sad figure. He had been barred from the club and pubs and only had the street kids to talk to.

Leatherman had to get to the disco, so Rowan came to the unit while we waited for the government contractors to take him. Being a good bloke, Rowan drove me home all the way to Glenorie.

The next week I had a funeral to arrange, a unit to sell and the usual family feud over who would get what. Aunty Doris, Ken's other sister, was in like a flash, after all the blood from his burst liver and shit everywhere had been cleaned up. Apparently the day before his death some street kids had tried to get an ambulance for him but he wouldn't go to the hospital. He knew it was his time, he was just tired of life and wanted to die in the little flat he loved.

The disastrous poker machine investigation down south was my last job as the token female with the Licensed Gamers for quite a long time. They made the regular Gaming Squad guys look good. Mind you, I do remember some enjoyable nights working with Karina from the Licensed Gamers. We would be given money to buy dinner, have a few drinks and watch the male strip shows. All we had to do for a day's pay was to write on the back of a coaster what the shows were: 'cowboy', 'fireman', etc. A couple of male officers would wait in the car park, just in case there was any trouble, and we would sit back and enjoy the spectacle. If any of the male strippers showed any pubic hair we just told the boys waiting outside, and they completed the paperwork for us. What a job! I should have paid them for the fun I had.

Mandy and I clicked well as a team as we were often prepared to go above and beyond the call of duty. One time she was sent into a brothel to apply for a job as a sex worker. Later at the debriefing she explained that during the interview she had been required to strip to pose for some erotic photos. Next thing, we were crashing through the door raiding the premises to recover the photographs. The boss wasn't having the possibility of photos of one of his officers ending up in court, or worse, the papers.

On another occasion I was involved in an operation with the National Crime Authority. My role was to accompany one of their undercover operatives to Diethnes, a Greek restaurant in Pitt Street that is still one of Sydney's culinary institutions. I was the blonde 'skip' girlfriend on the arm. They all spoke Greek while I ate and drank retsina. Again, I was being paid to go out and have a good time. Luckily there was no trouble, as I had gone numb from all the wine.

In October 1986, Mandy and I were set up in a motel near the beach at Bondi as part of the undercover investigation Operation Bank. Our mission was to infiltrate an illegal gaming house at Kings Cross. We befriended an old guy by the name of Ernie who ran the front counter. He gave us the job of working the security system to keep the cops out while illegal games were going on. At night I worked behind the front reception desk and pushed the buzzer to let those people who were allowed in through the steel door. My days were spent sunbaking on Bondi beach. I was getting paid more to work for the crooks than I was from the cops. It was a great couple of weeks.

After a few days Ernie took us upstairs to his room to show off all his stolen jewellery which he kept in a little wooden chest under his bed. One of his occupations was being a fence, and he had collected this lot after many years as his superannuation policy. I have never seen anything like it before or since. It was the best of the jewellery stolen from homes in the Double Bay–Edgecliff area. There was even a diamond tiara. Many of the items under the bed looked like family heirlooms, the sort that people would never be able to replace. It was all very valuable and, I imagined, traceable property. My family's home had been broken into and I knew what it felt like to lose irreplaceable family things. I was more interested in getting this stuff back to its owners than in a bunch of Lebs playing cards.

I was very apprehensive during the whole operation and eventually my worst nightmare happened. Late one night, Grimy Graham walked in while I was behind the counter.

He had come to the club looking to score some drugs. A bit of everything was going on at the club. I couldn't breathe with fear. When he saw me working behind the counter, he doubled up laughing. "Do they know they have a cop working for them?" he asked. "What are you doing here?"

"Working security to keep the cops out." This made him really start to lose it. I made him promise me he wouldn't tip them off. But he was a hopeless heroin addict, they would have paid him a lot of money for the information, and this was such a good story. I couldn't help thinking that if Graham gave them a telephone tipoff they would come out from the back and drag me away, never to be seen again.

Making an excuse to the manager of the club, I went up the road and rang my boss from a public telephone box. "I've been burnt by one of my old gigs who's just come to the club," I explained. "I don't think it's safe for me to keep going."

"Did you speak to him?"

"Yeah, I told him not to say anything. But I don't know if I can trust him."

"Too much money has been spent on this operation for us to quit at the first sign of trouble. Tell you what. Go back and finish your shift and give me a ring in the morning." I sensed he wasn't happy about being woken up.

On the way back to the club I noticed that I was trembling. My hands were moist with perspiration. *They are going to kill me*, I thought. I shuffled back, hoping I could disguise my feelings. I have heard it said that animals can smell fear. There were plenty of animals there that night.

The rest of the night was spent waiting for some big bloke to come and grab me and pull me out the back. But Grimy never tipped them off. A miracle that was, for which I am so thankful. He must have appreciated that I treated him like a human being. Maybe he had a heart still and took pity on a young girl that night.

The next night I called off sick and told them Mandy would work my shift. All the squad were put into position. When they hit the place Mandy opened the door and ran off down the street in fear, making it look as if it was an accident that she left the security door open. The club later wrote a letter of complaint to the police commissioner about how their staff member had been treated during the raid.

The raid was a success and the club was closed down. The detectives went up and searched Ernie's room, provided with a full description of where all the goodies were hidden. I don't know why he revealed his bounty to us, maybe it was pride or just showing off to two young girls. Surprise, surprise, the detectives came back and told us the box was empty. I still find it very strange that he had moved his superannuation policy out of the box to another place.

It was a close call and I look back now and think I would not want my daughters going into a den like that and just being left to their own devices. Operation Bank was primitive by today's standards, and it was pulled off through sheer luck rather than good management.

I later received a Commissioner's Commendation which was presented at Goulburn Police Academy by Commissioner John Avery. It reads:

Awarded to
CONSTABLE DEBORAH LEE WEBB
In recognition of
her outstanding dedication and resolve during the undercover operation 'Bank' undertaken in October 1986, which had as its target the gaming establishment known as the 'Barclay Club', Kings Cross
The Operation required Constable Webb to infiltrate the venue in order to obtain corroborative evidence, which meant considerable exposure to potential danger for lengthy periods. To her credit, the rigid security was overcome and the gaming establishment closed down.

I was very proud to be acknowledged for my undercover work. Police face danger every time they put a uniform on. Policing is an underpaid, thankless job for the most part. At the Police Academy they told us, "Never leave home fighting with your missus, as you may not come home at the end of the shift. You don't want their last memory with you to be of fighting." I am convinced cops really don't get paid enough.

The two boys at the Gamers, who spent most of their rostered shifts building fences, moved on to greener pastures around this time. Big Mark Menzies joined the squad from uniform duties. He was a former football player, about 1.9m (6 feet 4 inches) tall and he would have been fit in his day, but he had turned to fat. If he could go out of his way to do you a disservice he would.

Vivian West came in about the same time. She was tall with long red hair and blotchy skin. I knew she was very streetwise, having worked with her at North Sydney. She had told me her mother was white trash, like mine, but she herself adopted the image of a lady. She was a competent actress and the men fell for it.

I was a complete babe in the woods compared to Vivian. I liked to drink and be one of the boys too, but I couldn't organise my sex life the way she did. Casual sex always turned out to be more of an effort than it was worth, as I had to get home before daylight to check on Irene and John, not to mention feeding a kangaroo, chooks and four dogs. This meant that I rarely stayed a whole night with anyone.

But the biggest obstacle to an active sex life was that sex interfered with my drinking time. All the drinking required at the Gamers was starting to take its toll on me. Driving over the limit in a police car was never mentioned, nor were the other adverse effects of drinking so much alcohol. Nobody ever spoke to me about the damage being done from my working such long hours under the worst conditions possible. My life consisted of looking after Irene and John, going to work for long shifts, and drinking.

The Gaming Squad Surveillance Unit was a strange sight for a while, if you could work out what you were looking at. Lucas was doing his DJing and smoking a bit of grass. Mark was pissing off all the time to bonk the daughter of one of the bosses. Vivian was bulimic – she always took her toothbrush and lipstick with her to the bathroom – Mandy was fighting depression and I was on my way with the grog. Talk about a motley crew. But work was enjoyable. Most of our surveillance was spent sitting in pubs and off SP bookies' homes and we did have a good period when we all got on.

Lucas must have been delusional when he started spreading stories about his sexual conquests with the girls in the Gamers, including saying Mandy and I were hot for him. One afternoon I was doing paperwork with him in the surveillance room which was a little closet to one side of the office. We only ventured into the office occasionally to finish the paperwork and collect our meal claims. We were disrupted by the noise of one of the all-male teams arriving en masse. "Wait here, Deb," said Lucas. "There's something I want to talk to Glen about."

I was later told that Lucas had walked out of our office and through the intelligence area doing up his fly. "Debbie's in our office," he had told the others. "She doesn't want to come out as she will be too embarrassed." The boys thought it must be true. It wasn't long before Mandy was added to his long list of conquests. However, the wheels fell off his little red go-kart when he tried to tell all the boys that Vivian and I were having threesomes with him. The boss then politely asked him to find another place to work. Having contacts, in no time he was off again, swishing around in his leather pants.

Detective Sergeant Rowan Hutton finally won a cushy job, which he really deserved. It was the least they could do for the poor bastard. Mandy also moved to the Drug Squad. This left Mark in the driver's seat. However, he had been in one too many tackles and had no plain clothes experience. While he was in charge little work was being done. He was beginning to make sexual advances towards me, which I jokingly brushed off. As a result he turned nasty. Vivian was eager to encourage his animosity towards me, as she wanted to be the queen of the group. Giggling at all of Mark's nasty comments, she had obviously taken a dislike to me. I knew we were never going to be friends. Pretending I didn't care what they said, I thought they would get sick of going me. How wrong I was.

CHAPTER 7

MORE GAMES AT THE GAMERS

By early 1987, morale at the Gamers was not too good. The commander, Detective Inspector Fred Talley, an ex-first grade footballer, was still very fit for his age and had a bronze tan. He was a nice enough bloke but seemed old to me, being wrinkly and weatherbeaten from years of surf clubs and golf. Fred had a good heart, it just wasn't very big. He knew that things were really crook. The attitude of many of the investigators had gotten beyond a joke. Little work was being done and police cars were getting far too many dings from being driven by drunken coppers.

The floor was broken up into different territories by the men themselves. They fostered relationships. Ritcho, my old team sergeant, had the responsibility for looking over and targeting all the illegal Asian gaming houses. Sergeant Hudson dealt with the Greeks and Sergeant Cage had the Lebanese. Sergeant Crawford worried about the inner-city brothels.

By the mid 1980s the Gamers was in a hopeless situation. In fact it had probably always been off, but it was now becoming ridiculous. Many of the boys were just too greedy.

Everybody was so busy looking after their own interests that there was little time for police work. Just about every major player in illegal gaming was at least paying someone off in the office, so even those who were trying to do some work had their hands tied. Every time a raid was organised the boys would be jumping over each other to tip the crims off for drinking money or other favours.

It got to the point that when a raid was organised, none of the squad would be given any details prior to the doors being kicked in. This practice was not popular if you had a hot date and had just got back to the office to knock off, because we would be locked in. They even escorted me to the toilet. I'm not sure how they thought I was going to contact anyone from the toilet; perhaps I was supposed to send a message in a bottle. You couldn't even ring out to cancel your date. We would sit swearing in the office on overtime, and sometimes wait until 11pm before heading out on the raid. If we were lucky, some trusted servant would be sent out with petty cash to obtain McDonalds for the troops. So, bored shitless, we sat there eating cold McDonalds, debating who had been most put out.

Even after several successful raids, the bastards still found a way of knowing when we were coming. I don't know what the signal was, but someone was getting the drum to the gamblers.

One night the team was waiting in the office, catching up on our duty books and other backlogged paperwork. We were soon to go out again and sit off near the house of one of the targets we had been working on all week.

"Change of plans for tonight," chirped Mark, putting down the phone. "We're working on a job up at the Cross as a favour for the Licensing boys."

"What's the go?"

"We're going to sit off a brothel for a couple of hours. Apparently this joint is involved in importing young Asian girls as sex slaves. They're tricked into coming over here, their passports are taken away and they are forced to go on the game."

At first we went and sat off the Bondi home of the owner of the brothel. We left Lucas doing the eyeball. The rest of the team parked in neighbouring streets, then we all met up and sat in Mark's car. The inside was like a tip, smelling of decaying food and filled with McDonalds wrappers. Because it belonged to the cops, he never bothered to wash or clean it.

Little Joey, an Italian from down south, had now also joined the group. He knew that one day he would be working back down south with Mark, so he was always very careful to keep on his good side. Mark was so big and intimidating it would have taken a brave person to cross him in any way.

We were all pleased that Mark had stopped off at a bottle-oh on the way to the job and got some cold ones. He had beer for the boys and UDL cans for the girls. "Seeing we are going to be sitting around for bloody hours we may as well have a drink," he said. I was happy to have a couple of cans, and drank Vivian's, as she was always worried about calories.

After a few hours when the grog was all drunk, Mark moved us around to the brothel at the Cross. We sat squashed in his car again, swapping war stories as cops do. After a few more hours Mark was starting to look bored. "Time to go home, guys, stuff it. We did what they asked, there's no point hanging around here." We finished the cans we were drinking. I hate to think what we looked like – idiots sitting in a car drinking, I suppose.

We all got out of the car to stretch our legs and walk back to our own cars to go home. Mark slid up to me and started talking while the others left. We were both quite drunk and went for a walk up and down the strip. Of course we ended up in one of the sex shops. "How about it, Deb?" he asked as he pushed me into a booth.

"Piss off, Mark," I said. I was unsure how to handle the situation. He was such a big bastard and I had seen his foul temper so often. Undeterred, he went to the counter inside the sex shop and bought me the biggest vibrator they had. Maybe he was thinking that if he bought it for me I would give him a demo. He was sadly disappointed. With him still hanging off me, we returned to the cars with my brown paper bag. Not wanting to upset him further I pretended I was appreciative. The silly bastard had spent $60, which back in those days was a lot when you had a wife, kids, and another girlfriend to keep. I threw it out of the car window on the way home.

The next morning at the office Mark seemed to have the shits. From that day the verbal abuse started. He kept making horrible jokes about what a slut and bitch I was, and spreading stories. This went on and on. He seemed to have developed a pathological hatred towards me.

He really scared me on a trip back from Kiama. We were travelling back in convoy, talking on the police back channels between the cars. I was behind a big truck. The car in front would tell the next car behind when it was safe to overtake the truck. Mark was in the car in front of me. He called over the radio, "Go now!" I pulled out and came face to face with a semitrailer. Jerking the wheel hard to the left I managed to squeeze back into the lane with inches to spare. My scream must have nearly popped the speakers in the other vehicles. I could feel my pulse hammering against the sides of my skull.

"Oh, I said, 'Don't go now,'" came Mark's voice nervously across the air. "The radio must have cut out on the 'don't.'"

Joey, who was right behind me, said, "She was nearly splattered, why would you say that? It came over the radio to me as 'Go now.' Why would you have called that out?" Silence was the only reply. I still can't drive that stretch of road without a pain in my chest.

After that, it seemed that Mark would shake and glare whenever I came into a room – his anger smilingly fuelled by Vivian. A short time later we were away on another investigation in Queensland. On the second night at the hotel, Mark grabbed my head and smashed it into a big watermelon that was cut in half on the table. As he held my face down in the watery pulp I thought I was going to drown before he finally released me.

Too scared to make a fuss, I managed to slip away and told the story to my colleague whom I found swimming in the hotel pool. He just stared at me, which was disappointing, as I knew the boss had brought him onto the team in the hope that he could control Mark. Bob was a nice bloke, but Mark clearly intimidated him, and the two men had been fighting over the leadership of the unit. Mark Menzies just did not care what he did.

Not long after this Fred Talley made his best – or his worst – decision when he asked a former Internal Affairs officer to transfer to the Gaming Squad and sort out the Surveillance Unit. Detective Sergeant Kimbal Cook arrived on the Monday morning. Bob got the shits and just went back out on the floor. He was having a hard enough time fighting Mark for leadership of the section and he knew he was way out of his league when it came to Kim.

Kim was a handsome man in his thirties with gentle features. He was below the average height of most policemen but had stature in the way he carried himself. Although he was still young, his hair was noticeably turning grey. Kim was in for a challenge. Mark didn't like the idea of a new boy coming in and taking over his job, especially when the new boy was a detective sergeant while he was a senior constable. Doing what Mark did best, he started on his bully tactics.

Sutherland shire, which still has property within reach of a police salary (maybe because of its proximity to a nuclear reactor and its distance south of Sydney) is nicknamed 'Cop Land' after the movie starring Sylvester Stallone because so many police live down there. In the power struggle between Mark and Kim, Mark had the support of Joey, a uniform kid, also from down south, as well as support from Vivian, who liked loading the bullets and getting someone else to fire them. She would flutter her eyelashes, look soulfully out of her big blue eyes and swish her long hair and all the guys would respond accordingly.

The boss soon recruited Frank Deak, another sergeant from Internal Affairs, and Gene Zubrecky also joined the unit. Frank was a tall man, with thinning grey hair, a round face and sharp nose, who always wore baggy blue jeans and white runners. Gene looked like the Wild Man of Borneo with his long, matted shock of blonde hair and beard to match. Covered in tattoos, he would wear as little clothing as possible to show off the illustrations.

Kim Cook was the sort of cop I had always expected to find when I commenced plain clothes duties. Early on at one of the morning meetings the team was all seated at the conference table. "If you make a mistake I will go all out to help you," Kim began. "But if anyone here on my team does anything dishonest, corrupt, I will go out of my way to crucify you."

This is the sort of boss I want to work for, I thought. He seemed fair dinkum, honest, and just wanted to come to work to actually do his job. Kim was a married man who loved his wife and kids. He was a true gentleman, something I haven't come across very often during my career.

But now going to work was just bloody awful. You could cut the air with a knife. Mark was putting all his energies into doing a job on Kim. Every time Kim asked us to conduct surveillance of suspect premises, Mark's crew would just drive past and then go to the nearest pub, to spend the rest of the shift bitching about him as an act of defiance. They would write up bullshit in their duty diaries trying to bring Kim down, giving false information to make him look as if he was unable to run a successful operation. Kim was given no control or respect, but he refused to be intimidated.

In the end he went to the boss and told him that the situation was impossible. Fred gave Mark and Joey one week to find a transfer, and they went back to uniform down south. Vivian, however, after flashing her long painted eyelashes, was slipped into a detective's office and was saved from the embarrassment of returning to uniform. I heard that she left the force after a few more years.

Constable John Deerfield and Tracey Hall were brought in as replacements. John had deep brown eyes, olive skin and long dark hair flowing down over his shoulders. Tracey was physically well endowed with thick auburn hair and a warm smile.

I was now the last original member of the surveillance team. Although we worked under a boss who was fair dinkum, it was uncanny that as hard as we tried, every time we attempted surveillance on a gaming establishment, the bastards still knew we were there.

The surveillance operation on the two-up game in the shed just behind the Lane Cove National Park was about to step up a gear. Gene had gone off sick that night so we were down a member. Kim, thinking of ways not to have the surveillance 'burnt' by the targets, borrowed his brother's taxi and drove down the dirt road to the shed. There were about 200 players at the shed by this time. Posing as a taxi driver calling to pick up a fare, he pulled up outside the shed to get a look at the heads playing and the layout of the premises. Within seconds some of the organisers walked straight out of the shed and up to the taxi. "Did someone call for . . ." Kim began. Without any change in their expression two of the guys reached in and pulled him our of the car and onto the dirt.

"Pig," answered Kim's question at the same time as boots were thumping into his ribs. Immediately surveillance team vehicles careered into the clearing in a cloud of dust and gravel. Those dishing out the punishment, and the other gamblers, fled in all directions. Kim was left lying in the dust looking the worse for the experience. It was not the last hiding to be administered to Kim, but he was made of tough stuff.

(Around this time Kim confided to me that both his parents had also been alcoholics. He knew what a handful Irene and John were being. They were ringing me at work and demanding that I drive home and buy them a bottle of grog, as they were too far past it to get one for themselves. They were also constantly fighting while hiding their share of the flagon from each other. John would spend the day looking for the new hiding place, and then Irene would go ballistic when she found dribble down the side of her bottle.)

Most surveillance work is spent sitting in cars bored out of your mind while concentrating on not missing something. You may be waiting all day for someone to come back to a car left in a parking station. If you lose concentration on the 'eyeball', or nod off for a few seconds, you can miss the target and a whole day or even week's observations can be wasted. Whole weeks can be spent starting and finishing in the field without going into the office. You start feeling as if you live in your car. It becomes like a second skin. It's great when a target goes into somewhere like a shopping centre, so you can follow on foot for a while. When on surveillance we would eventually have to get back to the office to catch up on paperwork, report back to the boss and submit meal allowance forms to recoup the money we had spent on the takeaway food consumed in our cars.

I began to notice that Gene and Frank were often off to one side deep in conversation with wicked looks on their faces, but they would stop when they saw me coming. I'm sure they were deciding I was not to be trusted. They were right. Except for these occasions, they appeared to be a couple of the nicest guys. Gene's wife came and worked on the intelligence desk at the Gaming Squad. She was a charming, petite blonde and they seemed like the perfect police couple.

One Friday night about ten, Kim, with search warrant in hand, led us from the main road into the darkness of the lane behind a terrace in Surry Hills where we had been told a game was taking place. Gene swung the heavy sledgehammer, referred to as 'the key', at the deadlock on the back door, breaking it. We quickly followed Kim into the house, but instead of illegal gamblers we saw a group of people, including the solicitor Chris Murphy, standing by a long table covered with food under a large painted 'Welcome' banner.

"Good evening, ladies and gentlemen. Can we offer you something to eat?" they said.

Standing next to Mr Murphy was a young well-dressed Greek bloke with a video camera, obviously there to record our entry. The warrant was executed and the search didn't take long as there was absolutely no sign of any illegal gaming. Our video guy videoed their video guy videoing him. It was all a bit embarrassing.

After that debacle, around June 1988 we undertook a large operation on a well-known bookmaker, a big-time operator working out west. Our surveillance took us close to the border of Victoria and New South Wales. I was driving the lead vehicle with the rest of the team dropping back to avoid getting burnt. Not used to travelling at high speeds on country roads, I was relieved when we reached town. As I was the only one in 'the follow' at this point I wasn't going to let our quarry out of my sight. He was good at the anti-surveillance tactics. I couldn't find any of the other cops so I just kept going. He must have dismissed me as a tourist, presumably because I had tits. He went into what appeared to be a vacant office with black plastic on the glass.

I didn't take my eyes off the entrance to the office in case it was just a trick, not where he intended to take bets. I couldn't work out where the rest of the gang was. The town was not that big. Eventually out of the corner of my eye I saw bloody John sitting at a milk bar counter hoeing into a sandwich. I managed to attract his attention. "What are you thinking?" I said. "I've got him! He's a jumpy bastard. Go find the others." Just because *they* were out of the show, they must have thought I had lost him.

The bookmaker was later arrested and charged with gaming offences. Documents that supported the charges were found in the office. When he was on bail – he wasn't going to abandon his career just because he'd been arrested – we followed him again, this time in the Goulburn area. At that point I had to leave the operation and return to Sydney to sit a university exam.

Later I found I had missed all the excitement. Gene and Frank asked Kim if he was interested in a cut of the $10,000 bribe the bookmaker had just offered them. The next time they met, Kim had the negotiations secretly taped. Then, when all the arrangements for the exchange had been finalised, he contacted the Goulburn Highway Patrol to use as backup. The guys who end up in the Highway Patrol are a special breed. Other cops refer to them as 'cockroaches'; some of them would book their own mothers if it meant getting their quota up. They are the only members of the force who enjoy getting other cops for something.

Kim arranged to meet Frank and Gene in McDonalds, Goulburn, after they had received the bribe money. For some reason Frank and Gene decided to use my surveillance vehicle; I had left it behind when I returned to Sydney for the exam. As they arrived at the meeting point, the Highway Patrol was in place around the corner. With a glow of satisfaction on their faces they took Kim to the boot of the vehicle to view their efforts. Kim confirmed that the $10,000 was there and removed his baseball cap, the visual signal to the Highway Patrol officers.

Knowing nothing of this, I returned to the office the day after finishing my exam, just before 7am. The only other person in the office, Gene's wife, who was in tears. "What's wrong?" I enquired.

Between sobs she told me what happened. "Kim set them up," she growled. "The bastard." I thought, *Well, they had been warned. They knew the rules of the game.* Frank must have thought he could trust Kim, as they had worked together at Internal Affairs years earlier.

I asked Kim about it when he came back from the country. "Well, what could I do?" he asked. "How did I know it wasn't a setup? I have a wife and kids, a mortgage. What were they thinking? What choice did I have?"

Both men were sentenced to a gaol term. This did not help Kim's relationship with the Gaming Squad. The boss must have wished he had never brought Kim in. There wasn't much he could have done himself; the boys were now out of control. One morning as I walked through the office I saw some blokes from the floor sitting around in a group. Their dark expressions scared me; I could sense the mass hatred. Many of these guys had crossed the line themselves and they realised that if they had been in the wrong place at the wrong time, they might have joined Gene and Frank in the slammer. It didn't take me long to realise who they were talking about.

"Let's load the bastard up. Put some gear in his locker or car."

"Let's just get the cunt. We'll make it late at night, bash the shit out of him."

"Better still, a bullet in the head."

"Who the fuck does he think he is to do this to one of us?"

"We'll have to fix this. He'll have to be made an example of."

I kept walking. As a member of Kim's team I felt as if I had been tarred with the same brush, even though I hadn't been involved in the arrests. Just supporting Kim was a social death sentence.

If possible, the air grew even thicker with hostility as the days passed. I couldn't stand the thought of having to face it every morning. A cartoon drawing of John Deerfield being hanged and stabbed was pinned to an office wall. Anonymous phone calls were being received by members of the team. These seemed to warn of things to come.

About six weeks after the arrests at Goulburn I walked into Fred's office. "I can't stand this any more," I informed him. "It's too scary for me. Someone is going to get hurt the way it's going and I don't want it to be me. I want out."

"I think you're a smart girl. Debbie," he told me. "You're better off away from all this. I have a friend at Parramatta. He owes me a favour, and I'll give him a ring right now. I know I can get you out there."

About an hour later he said, "It's all arranged. You start at Parramatta Detectives' office on Monday morning. You won't have so far to travel either."

"Thanks, Fred."

I felt guilty that I was running out on Kim, John and Tracey, but the whole thing scared me. For two cops to be arrested was a dangerous precedent that could not be allowed to continue, and these guys were looking for revenge. If you didn't agree with something you were supposed to look the other way; Kim had broken the code that said loyalty to the brotherhood was the most important thing.

CHAPTER 8

A NEW BEGINNING

I started at Parramatta on 29 July 1988. The office was much longer than it was wide, which made it seem more like a corridor than a place of work. An external wall was nearly all windows which meant that we would all fry in the hot afternoon sun. I was positive that everybody in Parramatta Detectives would know why I had been transferred so suddenly. To my surprise everyone was very friendly. It was the only time in my experience that the grapevine hadn't arrived ahead of me.

My new partner was Ron Marowitz, who immediately took me under his wing. I discovered later that this was because his brother Jim had previously been in the Gaming Squad, and had told the boys what a party it was. The Gamers was a tough squad to get into; you had to be invited to join the club, so the blokes at Parramatta thought I was cool. They might also have assumed I jumped ship because of the Gene and Frank affair, when in actual fact I had run because I wasn't interested in receiving payoffs from crims. Unfortunately, I was far from cool.

Ron Marowitz was a slimy, skinny, pock-faced little weasel whose brother Jim was famous for sailing pretty close to the wind and had shammed his way out of the force when things got hot. He was widely admired, which amazed me.

The detective inspector in charge of the office was known as 'Whitey'. Over his large beer gut he often wore a crumpled white shirt which invariably had cigarette ash down one side. He was a nice old bloke but although he was interested in what was happening on the floor he would rarely venture out of his office. "Only two years and two months to retirement," he would say.

Detective Sergeant Mitch Krankel was the other old bloke in the office in the same boat. I was the only one who liked him. He was constantly ridiculed due to his German accent. I don't know how he survived all those years either, not being an Aussie. When the guys got pissed on night work they would rip up his briefs of evidence, superglue the locks on his filing cabinet and place bricks in his drawers. On several occasions they even damaged his car in the police parking lot. I would think to myself, *He is one of us. What the hell are you doing this for?* But of course he was different, he was not one of the boys, he was honest. Sadly, he spent his last days in the job counting down the days till he retired, like Whitey.

The rest of the office seemed a bit scary. Ron Marowitz and Lloyd Grigg had senior partners, both of whom had left Parramatta and gone to other sub-stations to get away from

Internal Affairs pressure. Ron and Lloyd had taken over their territories, yet they weren't really in command as they reported in on the telephone every day to their old mentors.

I had to learn a few things to bring myself up to speed. One was that as a detective the biggest status symbol you can have is to run a second home. Then you know you have really made it. It earns great respect from the other men. I got used to sitting in the car while one of the blokes had a quick bonk during his shift with Wife No. 2. Once I actually received an invitation inside. I could only assume No. 2 had knocked him back that time. He looked like the doting dad, grabbing his little ten-month-old boy and throwing him up over his head. I almost saw a human side to him.

When we had finished there we went on a long drive to the outer suburbs to meet someone he referred to as 'the dragon'. She turned out to be his wife, a frumpy housewife not in the least like the little sexy nineteen-year-old we had just left. I nearly choked on my coffee when he brought out an almost identical ten-month-old boy, with the same nickname, and started flying him around his head as well. When we got back in the car I asked, "Why do you call them both the same name?"

"They were born only two weeks apart," he said. "I don't want to call either of them by the wrong name. My guts would be garters."

Danny was another colourful character. He was tall and fat, reeking of garlic, with a big red face, a loud voice and the habit of being in your personal space. He wore beige tailored pants that were too small with shiny nylon shirts stretched to the seams. Ron worked for Danny in his spare time as a concreter. This was also a front for the extra money he had.

Danny was a 'runner' – a go-between with many duties – for Louis Bayeh. He usually had large amounts of money and wasn't afraid to flash it around. He often took all the detectives out for lunch or dinner and paid for the whole meal. Sometimes he would ring up the office after being on the drink all day and demand a lift home. Somebody would have to race out and get a detective's car to pick him up. "He treats us like a bloody taxi service," they complained, but they were under obligation to him because he had paid for so many lunches.

Danny took a fancy to me, and I was very angry when Ron gave him my home phone number. The next time we met, he tried to put a wad of notes into my hand. "What is this for?" I asked.

"It's because I like you so much," he said with a grin. "Just take it, there's plenty more where that came from."

I told him he could stick his money where the sun didn't shine. "That's not the way to speak to Danny," I was told. "We have to keep him on side." I just shrugged and went back to my desk. I wasn't particularly worried about offending Danny. I didn't owe him any favours and wasn't about to start.

After I had been at Parramatta for a while Frank Deak and Gene Zubrecky had to face court proceedings. I was told that if the boys went to jail a contract would be put out on Kim's life. I went to Kim with this information and could see how badly the stress was affecting him. He had aged. He was frightened for himself and his family, and had every reason to be. He must have been thinking of what happened to Michael Drury who, like him, had two little girls. Undercover Detective Michael Drury had been shot twice through his kitchen window on 6 June 1984, and Roger Rogerson had been implicated with Christopher Dale Flannery – Mr Rent-a-Kill. Drury had been shot for a lot less than Kim Cook had done.

I have never heard a police officer say anything positive about Kim Cook. The young police were told that Deak and Zubrecky were good blokes and that Kim was a creep who needed to be paid back. I feel guilty that I did not remain at the Gamers with Kim, but I made a mistake in believing life would be safer in Divisional Detectives.

CHAPTER 9

BREAKING AND ENTERING

Ron and Lloyd appeared to have been given a free hand to do as they wanted. They would go out at the beginning of a shift and no one would ever ask what they were doing or where they were going. They spent much of their time in hotels and restaurants with informants. Lloyd liked to see how many free drinks and meals we could consume in a shift. He also received a double pass to movies at Parramatta each week. They thought he was keeping an eye on the place for them, so he really panicked when they were broken into.

I didn't like being Ron's partner. During my time with him I had seen a few things that concerned me, including soliciting and accepting free meals in restaurants around the Parramatta area, many with well-known crime identities. The night Ron took me to a meeting at a dark old picture theatre, I was feeling particularly ill at ease. There were people there I didn't know, some of whom were certainly not cops. After initial greetings they were all whispering about who knew what. Ron seemed always to have something on the boil. He sometimes took me to one of the brothels run by Louis Bayeh's brother Billy and left me sitting in the waiting room with the clients and the girls nobody wanted. This was not my idea of a great shift.

I heard a lot of rumours about money changing hands. Wherever we went to talk, or whisper business, he would always emphasise to the crooks and the other cops: "You can trust her, she's from the Gaming Squad." I was also offered money by Ron several times, but refused.

After coffee on the morning of Tuesday 2 August 1988, I asked Ron what the plan of attack for the day would be. "What's first, chief?"

"We are going to do a break and enter," he said.

Ron drove, as he told me I was still learning my way around. I suspected this was a male ego thing, or distrust of female drivers. Whatever, I was content to be chauffeured. "It's a bit out of Parramatta's patrol, but that's OK," Ron assured me. "This bloke is an old friend of mine. We went to school together."

Ron drove us to a town house in Carlingford. A tall dark-haired man answered the door. Invited into the lounge room, Ron dictated which details were necessary to place in my official police notebook concerning the bust. I carefully recorded the items alleged to have been stolen from the garage, as this was the first such investigation I had conducted as a detective.

We then walked around to the garage at the rear of the premises. The garage door was open and a flashy Mercedes-Benz was sticking halfway out. It was an older model in an unusual shade of blue. Unable to squeeze past the car to gain entry to the garage, Ron and this bloke stood outside and chatted quietly for what seemed like half an hour, just out of my hearing. I was left standing outside the garage door like an idiot. This was my first real divisional detective's job. *How boring*, I thought.

When we returned to the station Ron told me how to complete the investigation report forms, which were in triplicate. I was typing the form on an Olivetti electric typewriter, a luxury after years of sore fingers and broken nails using the old manual ones. Before I joined the Police Force there was a radio car on every night shift, in every division. A young plain clothes officer would sit in the back seat and type all the messages that came over the police radio on a manual typewriter. I was glad those days were gone. Not least because I can get very carsick.

When it came to the little box that had to be ticked for 'how entry gained' I asked, "How'd they get into the garage?"

"Um, with a screwdriver. Just put an x in that box."

I submitted the completed form via the tray on Whitey's desk and thought no more of it.

About seven months later I was partnered with Lloyd Grigg. We were walking from the Parramatta police station for a drink at one of our favourite spots, the Park Royal hotel. I saw the bloke whose house we had been to drive slowly past us in the same blue Mercedes I had seen in August. He gave us a good hard look. "Do you know who that is?" asked Lloyd.

"Yes."

"Oh, you weren't supposed to know that he's Ron's brother." I was stunned.

We were at the Park Royal before I could speak again. The way Grigg made his comment indicated he knew all about the break and enter report. I couldn't believe that this bloke was really Jim Marowitz. They had tipped me into a bogus break and enter for my first job. They had used me as soon as I walked through the door. *The bastards.* I was angry, and also very worried.

Because I was ex-Gaming, in Ron's book that made me one of the boys. At that time I also had my country girl personality too. I was easygoing, cheerful and laid-back with an open attitude. Ron thought I would just go along with him because I laughed at the boys' dirty jokes. He was trying to get something on me, get me involved and establish me as one of the boys so I could never put them in.

One evening I had a standup fight with him. When I challenged him about a rumour that Louis Bayeh had offered him $5000 to find and charge his opposition in the drug trade, he became very defensive. He didn't realise that what really upset me was spending the night running around Lakemba chasing a desperate drug dealer on behalf of another crook. Just Lloyd and I, and no one else knew where we were. If we had found him that night, who knows what might have happened? Ron didn't even understand why I was upset. These guys were on a totally different wavelength.

When I first started working with Lloyd Grigg, it was obvious Detective Sergeant Paul Diamond was not very happy. He dictated business to Lloyd, not the other way around. An unknown quantity like me was not part of the deal.

Lloyd was fun-loving and I enjoyed working with him. However, there were still many meals with Louis Bayeh. Lloyd fell short of being as big-time as he thought he was. He just found himself in situations from time to time. Having been trained by Diamond, he had bought the culture of sticking by your mate. Proud of sporting the leather jacket Louis Bayeh had bought him from a Lebanese leather shop in Parramatta, Lloyd actually showed me about five expensive new leather jackets at his home one day. Sometimes on afternoon shift we would work as debt collectors for the shop, chasing up people who were late on repayments.

Louis always seemed to enjoy my company. "Come with me for a holiday to Germany," he offered late one evening.

"No, thanks. You're a married man, aren't you?"

"That doesn't matter. Come on. It'll be fun."

"Sorry, Louis, I haven't any spare holidays."

It felt like the guys I was working with held me up as a token to offer the crooks, so they could rack up points with them. The young blonde policewoman they might be able to crack onto. Ron had already given my home telephone number to Danny, who wanted to take me out to dinner. In exchange for free meals and drinks my number was also given to another shady character who owned two restaurants in the area. He was also very keen on the idea of dating a policewoman. I quickly put him straight. I complained about all this, but got nowhere.

The Parramatta Detectives' car would be used every morning to pick up two staff members from the Parramatta Leagues Club and take them to the bank with the previous day's takings, with the police acting as security. "Why are we doing this?" I remember asking.

"Because they kick into the slush fund for it," was the reply.

The big mid-year BBQ and piss-up was apparently paid for out of these funds. Thousands of dollars were spent on food and grog, most of which came from providing unauthorised community services. From time to time Lloyd and I would work behind the bar at the Leagues Club for football games, supposedly watching staff who were alleged to be embezzling money. The scheme was really about Lloyd earning extra cash money as a second job. Paid in kind as well as cash, we consumed plenty of free drinks.

I was doing yet another shift with Lloyd on the grog. His fiery redhead of a girlfriend was jealous of the time we spent working together, thinking I was sleeping with him behind her back. Lloyd and I were just having fun, but it wasn't going to last. Basically Lloyd was a good bloke, just greedy. I guess most corrupt police start off just being good blokes.

Doing the usual rounds, we were getting quite tanked. We were stopped at some traffic lights when Lloyd looked over the left shoulder of one of his many leather jackets. "Look at that fuck ugly sheila!" he exclaimed.

"That's got to be a bloke in drag."

"No way. Wheel her over and let's find out."

It felt like we were always doing things like this. As the traffic lights changed we did the lights, sirens, the whole bloody lot, and the car pulled over. Using the correct police suspect vehicle procedure, we pulled up behind it slightly off centre to the right. We swanned up to the car, "Licence please, miss," requested Grigg. A coy look was the only reply.

Lloyd opened the driver's door, pulled her out and threw her up against the bonnet. "I'm on my way to a fancy dress party," she said. I had won the bet when she started to speak; it was a bloody bloke. "That's why I don't have my licence."

As it was 1am on a Wednesday night we concluded this was bullshit. "Go ahead and search the car, Deb," directed Grigg.

In the front, a half-drunk can of beer was next to a wet cloth. Something didn't seem right. I reached under the front seat and pulled out a sawn-off shotgun. "Fuck! Look at this," I yelled, sobering up immediately. As the words left my lips Lloyd pulled out his revolver, jamming it against the drag queen's temple. "Call for backup," Grigg instructed me. I ran back to the car and contacted police radio, requesting urgent assistance. What had started as a joke had suddenly turned deadly serious.

The paddy wagon arrived quickly with two fresh-faced boys on board. Grigg liked to do things by the book when the need arose, which was good. With the help of the extra hands I continued the search of the vehicle. I found an axe, a syringe full of blood and a bag with a note that read: 'This is a holdup. The gun is not for you. But the axe and the syringe full of aids blood is. Give me all your money or I will kill you.'

The poor bastard wouldn't stop crying, even after we drove him back to the station. He looked quite pathetic with mascara running down his face. Lloyd adopted his usual line of interrogation. Standing the suspect in the garbage bin he proceeded to punctuate his questioning by hitting him with the A–K telephone book. This helped him recall his correct name and finally his address. It appeared he was just driving around the block, having a can of beer for courage before holding up the garage on the next corner. How unlucky is it to be interrupted on a crime spree to settle a bet about your sexuality?

After the interview we called by his home. The loud police-style knock on the front door abruptly woke his poor wife. There is something about the way police knock on someone's door that makes people think, *Who the fuck is that? Sounds like trouble.*

The bloke's wife looked surprisingly attractive for that time of the morning, wearing only a white satin dressing gown. Grigg, all class and style, made her take it off and bend over naked to prove she was not hiding any concealed weapons. I could tell that he thought this was very smooth. As we ripped the house apart in true police fashion, we found the detached end to the sawn-off shotgun out by the little aluminium shed. She told us her husband had sawn it off earlier that night. "We used to own a factory," she explained. "But we got into serious financial trouble about twelve months ago because of his cocaine habit." She further explained he had insisted that she dress him up like a woman and put on a wig. He even got her to do his makeup. He wouldn't tell her where he was going, but you wouldn't have to be Einstein to work it out.

Grigg saw the wife again when stupid went to court. She was living in a caravan park with some new loser. From a life of luxury to being trailer folk had been a big comedown. But apparently she was happier. Almost anything looks better after life with a druggie.

We received a ton of overtime out of that job. You don't need it, however, because by the time the sun comes up you're really starting to feel crook. Talk about a lot of paperwork.

Out cruising late with Grigg, I could see police lights coming over the horizon. It was about 4am and there were no other cars around except the one trying to outrun the paddy wagon. "They must be chasing that car," I suggested to Grigg, stating the obvious.

"Nothing's come over the radio."

"I'm going to block the road."

"No bloody way."

Immediately leaping the median strip I angled the police car across the three lanes, Lloyd's side facing the oncoming vehicle. The car, trying to avoid a collision, still managed to clip us and sailed up the footpath, crashing into a wooden fence.

I jumped out in my usual tight straight skirt and stilettos that I wore to work. I looked good, even though Ron's name for me was Phar Lap. (He reckoned I had an arse on me like a horse.) Grigg quickly passed me on his way after the bloke who had leaped from the driver's seat. I throttled up to the car to discover it was packed full of marijuana plants.

The uniform guys went running after Grigg. Right under the passenger's side dash, a kid of about sixteen was curled up in a ball, trying to hide. Pumping with adrenalin by this time, I pulled him out by the hair and threw him on the ground. A bloke came from nowhere and was holding the kid down for me and, thinking he was from the Anti-Theft Squad, I yelled for his handcuffs. His stunned silence made me realise he was just a good citizen out for a stroll who had stopped to help me hold the young suspect down.

We got our boy back to the station and Lloyd took him up to the Detectives' office for a little interrogation involving the garbage bin and the Yellow Pages. We soon found out that our boy had also had two little mates in the car, and who they were. They had just ripped off some guy's plants when the neighbours had phoned in to complain of them being in the backyard. When the paddy wagon was chasing them, the officers hadn't even had time to call it over the air before I blocked the road. That's what I love about the job. One minute you're bored with nothing to do but cruise, the next you wouldn't know what was going to happen.

It was a nice spring evening in October 1988. Sitting in the office, we were attempting to get through more of the relentless paperwork. The old AWA speaker on the wall monitoring the local police channel for the office crackled out a request for a detective's vehicle to attend a motor vehicle accident at a domestic. "This is not good," I called to Grigg. "Something bad has happened. We better take the torches. It'll be dark soon."

He disagreed about the torches and I propped down there in my stilettos.

It was surreal.

When we got to the scene we were informed that some local white trash were having a piss-up, and had been having booze home delivered because they were too pissed to go out. However, the husband started to turn nasty with the wife and it had led to violence, so the cops were called. One of them was Constable Brett Sinclair, who once worked at the local Galston bottle shop frequented by my parents. My old man had always encouraged him to join the police after seeing how well I was doing, and he had recently been transferred to Parramatta. Like the other cops there, he didn't yet have much experience.

The troublemaking husband was revving the drink delivery truck that he drove for a living. He yelled out, among other things, "I'm gonna kill myself a cop. Piss off or I'll ram the truck!" One of the young cops decided to move the paddy wagon just in case, so he wouldn't have to do the paperwork if the paddy wagon got dented.

The bloke with the loud mouth started to back out of the driveway. Brett jumped up onto the driver's door and tried to pull the keys from the ignition. "I'm gonna kill you!" screamed the drunken fool. He then proceeded to plough the side of the truck into a tree. Brett's leg was almost ripped from his body. Crushed, he died almost instantly. I knew we should have taken our torches.

Lloyd and I booked the body into the morgue. The following day we attended the ID parade to have his body formally identified prior to the post mortem. I was shaken to be there with someone I knew not only as a great young bloke but also as a young man from where I lived before he joined the cops. Brett was a good, honest young guy who loved being a cop. I remembered giving him some tips before he joined the job. We got good and pissed at the Friend in Hand hotel, Glebe, after the autopsy.

A few months later when I was awarded the Commissioner's Commendation down at Goulburn Police Academy from my time at the Gaming Squad, Brett's wife was there too. She was a young policewoman, there to accept his posthumous award for bravery.

I didn't know what to say. What can you say?

Another sad thing happened earlier that day, while I was

waiting for Mandy to turn up so we could drive down together to get our awards. She had been in the Undercover Drug Squad but had ended up too far under the covers. After playing pool in a pub all night she had walked on broken glass, cutting the bottom of her feet. She was off her face as I sat in the office trying to get her shoes on. Mandy's assignment was to have gotten close to a major drug dealer. A couple of months later they asked how she was going. She was very happy, thank you very much, as she was now living with him full time.

I saw Mandy only once more after that. She had been told to resign, as she had become a hopeless addict. There was no talk of rehabilitation in the early 1990s. Years in the Drug Squad had taken their toll on her. Mandy had tried Narcotics Anonymous but she believed it could work for everyone but her. She ended up a very sad story, another piece of wreckage from the New South Wales Police.

Lloyd and I partied a lot, and sometimes time got away on us. Before we knew it, our shift would be over. Still having to justify our existence, we had an arrangement with one of the local pawnshops. We would sit out the back looking through the one-way mirror, occasionally having a quiet drink with big Jimbo the owner. Eventually he would give us someone, a druggie usually, who was not a regular. Some poor bastard who was lost to society. One day a pathetic excuse of a human being came in weighing about forty kilos. He was gently laying out a horse saddle and stirrups from his pet horse that had died. We just walked out from the back and grabbed him by the arm, placing him in the back of the unmarked police car. He was too sick to even protest and only wanted another hit. By the time we got back to the station, the saddle had been reported stolen from a garage.

Grigg and I also fostered informants. One poor bastard gave up his local dealer. We hit him the next morning with a search warrant. Lloyd knocked on the door and this bleached blonde answered the door. We pushed past and searched the back of the fridge. Alas, no gold.

We then began searching the rest of the house, which resulted as usual in the place being turned upside down. However, you wouldn't have noticed the difference in this place. Finding some bullets, Lloyd told me to be on guard. In the main bedroom I opened the wardrobe door, only to have a big pair of bulging eyes jump out at me from the darkness. I screamed just as a blond, long-haired druggie dressed only in little tight black undies jumped back into the wardrobe, slamming the door shut.

Lloyd found me unable to speak, pointing at the wardrobe. He pulled the bastard out, threw him on the bed and laid into him. "What did I do?" whimpered the suspect. "What was that for?"

"Scaring a policewoman. That's what for."

We had the dog go through the place, but there were no drugs to be found. Our informant must have tipped him off that we were coming.

Lloyd's main occupation in the Police Force was protecting a young lady named Mary. Her parents lived in a fibro Housing Commission house in Wentworthville, an outer western suburb. Mary had grown up in the house and at some stage while still at school, she fell in love with the boy next door. Unfortunately he was a psychopath.

He had told her he would kill her if they broke up, so she'd suffered many years of intimidation without anyone knowing. For two days she didn't tell her mother about a broken collarbone. The truth finally came out that he had hit her with a motorbike helmet.

This bloke, whom I'll call Jethro, was not happy about being unable to see his true love any more. This guy was very clever and had learned to make listening devices out of Tic Tac boxes after studying electronics at TAFE. He started bugging the house so he could hear what his Mary was up to.

One day a visitor's little boy kicked a ball under their fibro house. When he came out from getting the ball he asked why they had a phone under their place. Jethro had wired up a phone there so he could listen to Mary's phone calls. Another time the family discovered that he was trying to carve out the inside of their lounge so he could hide in it.

Every time they went out, old Jethro would break in and do a bit of a ransack through the place. Lloyd found an airbed and tins of food in the ceiling space in Mary's bedroom; lover boy had drilled a small hole in the roof so he could watch her sleeping. Lloyd became emotionally involved when he started sleeping with Mary after spending so much time going back and forth to their home. He really cared for her but Jethro found out Lloyd's home address and started telephoning him there. That spooked him, but he still tried to do all he could for her. I think he took it so personally because Jethro had actually unsettled him.

Many court cases and two admissions to psychiatric hospitals did not deter Jethro from the pursuit of his true love. If he couldn't have her, neither would anyone else. During one of his admissions to hospital he escaped, kidnapped Mary and held her in a shed in the grounds of the hospital for three days before they were discovered. Another time he held the parents captive with a carving knife. Her sister Brook kept a file of all the incidents, and it was as thick as a phone book.

When I arrived on the scene one day, Ryde police had just caught Jethro creeping around in the long grass near the sister's house. Lloyd was notified of the incident. This meant more coffee with the sister and Mary as he had a genuine concern for the whole family. We could not work out what Jethro was up too.

A couple of weeks later the phone rang. Lloyd answered it and I saw the blood drain from his face. He got up from the other side of the desk and just waved his hand to indicate we were going somewhere. In the car he told me, "Jethro has struck again. The bastard!"

When we arrived at the sister's house I could not believe the scene before me. Large carving knifes were protruding though the backs of all the dining room chairs. GI green cordial had been poured over the white carpet all through the house and through the clothes in the wardrobes. I found the video recorder in the bottom of the pool. "He's just getting worse each time," said Brook. "How can anybody protect us from this psycho?"

Lloyd took all this very personally. Back at the office we obtained a search warrant for Jethro's joint. He had now moved into a flat at the back of a house at Petersham. Lloyd explained to Whitey what we were up to, informing him that it would be a long night. Whitey said it was okay. Overtime approval never appeared to be a problem if you had a job on.

Indian food being one of my favourites, Lloyd introduced me to a restaurant on Parramatta Road, one he had cultivated over a long period of time. When the owner saw him walk through the door he got a tired look on his face and pulled out a bottle of port. Here he was, being hit for another free feed by the constabulary. After a fantastic meal, off we went to lock up Jethro.

As quietly as possible we walked down the side of the house to his flat at the rear. After a short, loud knock on the door Lloyd started to kick it in. With the warmth of the port in his gut he was ready for action. I stood back like the girlie I was meant to be while it took him some time to break the seal. Jethro was not home. We were surprised to find he had a red light sensor in his bedroom to let him know when someone came down the side of the house. This guy was a technical genius.

We started searching for green GI cordial. Talk about smart, we found overalls, shoes and undies all soaking in a tub of water and detergent. Later forensic examination came up with nothing.

By the time we had finished, Jethro's place looked like Brook's, and Lloyd was really foaming at the mouth. We went to the pub to fill in a few hours. After several beers Dave told me that after he had seen Mary one night he came out in the morning to find his four-wheel-drive broken into, with the garden hose hooked up and the sprinkler going inside. I could see why Lloyd had more than just a professional interest in dealing with Jethro. He was really going to be in for it if Lloyd could get his hands on him. At about 1am we went back to Jethro's house to find his poor old mum and his sister cleaning up the mess we had made. There were lots of victims in this tragedy.

Mary's name was eventually changed and she was moved overseas. She was told not to make contact with her family as Jethro might be able to track her down. This was a big price to pay, but it was only a matter of time before he killed her. It's scary to think that if someone decides to make your life a misery, you cannot be really protected. There are other Jethros out there doing their stuff right now.

The turning point for me at Parramatta Detectives' office was the day Ron went down for a big lunch, leaving me sitting in the bloody office like an idiot. Ron called me up a few hours later and told me to walk down to the Park Royal hotel. It was only a couple of blocks from the station. So I wandered down in my high heels and tight skirt. (I had a real figure in those days. The nails and the hair were also always immaculate.)

I found Ron with Louis Bayeh. Lennie McPherson was there too; I recognised him after having worked surveillance on him at the Gamers. I was surprised; this must be a big meeting. I had been brought up on Lennie stories as my uncles had worked on the docks. One uncle had even worked for him as a youth while hiding stolen motors for him in his garage near Lennie's house at Gladesville. I smiled sweetly, waiting to find out what was going on.

Ron invited me out to talk in the front of the Park Royal entrance. From his pocket he pulled a folded piece of paper. It was a gun application in the name of McPherson's wife, and it looked as if they had filled it out over the boozy lunch. I didn't know what to make of this. Could they possibly expect to pass this over and get it? Was it a trap to set me up? Not knowing what to say I fell back on my usual response and just laughed. These days I would have shoved it down his throat. "You have got to be joking," I insisted. "There is no way in the bloody world I'll take this to a police station and pay it."

Ron was looking irritated. "Well, if you don't want to do it, get one of your girlfriends to."

"No way in hell."

Ron pulled out a wad of money. "How much do you want?"

"Fuck off, Ron."

What was in this for me kept going up and finally reached about $150. It was a lot for a five-minute job, but no amount would have been enough. Ron was beginning to sweat; he didn't want to go back into the hotel with the licence application still on him. What I should have done was taken the bloody thing as evidence. Instead, I gave it back to him with my fingerprints all over it.

After that day I couldn't rest, thinking, *Well, they have really got me now.* I didn't know what to do, who to turn to. The whole of Parramatta was off. I believe the saying that for evil to grow, it only takes people of goodwill to do nothing.

I was on the brink of making the biggest decision of my life so far, to rat them out. What really pushed me over the edge was one particular night with Ron. We had been to a brothel in

Granville, then we cruised by to a gaming establishment. All they had to drink was beer and scotch. I hate both, so it was a real pain being there. Ron went out into the back room to play Chinese whispers for what seemed like hours. On his return I was nearly falling asleep watching the old men play cards.

We then just sat in the back lane and listened to the police radio. Calls kept coming over for one particular cop, stating that his wife had been abducted. Ron explained that this was a warning for this cop as they were worried that he was thinking about putting them all in. He had been giving some of their people a hard time and this was just to show him what was to come if he kept annoying them. I felt like I was going to vomit. He had the biggest threat sitting right next to him, although he didn't have a clue.

CHAPTER 10

CROSSING AGAINST THE LIGHTS

I thought for a long time about telephoning Kim Cook to ask for his help about Parramatta. He was the only honest cop I was sure of, the only one I could trust. My parents' opinion of the predicament I found myself in was very much in the forefront of my mind. My mother's advice still rings clear. "Keep your head down, girl," she said, as if she had seen it all. "You're in the big league now ... These boys don't muck around. You don't fuck with Roger Rogerson. You saw what happened to Michael Drury. Just smile and be sweet."

What sort of advice was this? Her daughter had found herself associating with major criminal identities, as a Parramatta detective, and she thought I was doing very well, thank you! Poor Irene had no idea. She had been a switched-on gal in her day, but now she was just in an alcoholic haze. Only another cop could understand the situation I was in.

Of biggest concern at the time was that if I didn't take action I might end up in gaol, or worse. The instinct for self-preservation was becoming urgent. I just wanted to be a cop and do my job properly. By attempting to compromise me, the bastards weren't letting me do that.

One night in April 1988 I finally made the decision to ring Kim. It was a gut-wrenching choice. I knew what a considerable step this was. I was terrified, heading into uncharted territory. I recalled what had happened to Phil Arantz, how he had spoken out about falsified police statistics. How he had been grabbed and locked up in a mental institution. The doctor who certified him to be admitted to the institution had been Dr Morrie Vain, the same doctor who physically examined me when I applied to join the police.

It was not lost on me that Drury had been shot through his kitchen window while washing up. He had also upset some dangerous people. He hadn't even spoken out about corruption until after he was shot. He was shot with a magnum revolver; the only thing that saved his life was that one of the bullets ricocheted off the curtain rod. The near-fatal wounding occurred in front of his wife and two young girls. Irene and John were like my children. If something happened to me there was no one to look after them. They had very high needs. The district nurse would come around to the house and help me with them, but I was the only one who could keep them under control. They were totally reliant upon me for everything.

I telephoned Kim at home. "Can you meet me at that coffee shop in Oxford Street? I'm having problems at Parramatta and you are the only person I can talk to."

Kim was already seated in the small cafe as I arrived. It wasn't one of the newer renovated cafes, but it was private. He looked older and very tired. The past few months had taken a big toll. After we ordered cappuccinos, I detailed to Kim all about the break and enter incident and everything else that was going on at Parramatta. While I spoke he sat almost motionless, head down, contemplating his coffee.

Kim waited until I had finished. I talked for ages, telling him every minor detail. I do that. I needed to paint the entire picture so he would understand how serious this all was. He understood. He had been around a lot longer than I had and knew the score.

"What else can you do?" he said after a pause. "You need to take your story to IPSU."

The Internal Police Security Unit sounded like the right place. I'd seen Cook take a stand against corruption and do the right thing at the Gaming Squad. I still felt guilty that I had chosen to leave the Gamers when things became dangerous. Maybe I could have supported him more if I had stayed. I was impressed with his courage and I respected what he'd done. If I made a stand and just told them the truth I would be all right, wouldn't I? Having all the evidence about the break and enter, surely they should believe me. What could go wrong if I went to the top, to the Internal Police Security Unit, and told them the truth?

"Make a chronology of events. If you make a list then you won't leave anything out when you make your complaint." Kim finished his coffee. "Leave it with me. I'll make arrangements and give you a ring. I'll come to the meeting with you if you like."

Having confided in someone who understood what I was talking about made me feel much better. However, the dread in the pit of my stomach wouldn't shift. I was very young and could be naive about things, especially about the NSW Police Force. A harsh lesson in reality was on its way.

One April evening I had just arrived home when the phone rang. It was Kim, asking me to meet him outside the Graphic Arts Club at about ten the following morning. The Graphic Arts Club in Regent Street near Central station was a popular watering hole for police coming off night shift, as you could always get a drink there. Every cop in Sydney knew to be careful when leaving the club intoxicated because the IPSU was in the old Regent Street police station across the road.

I was running late. Kim was waiting for me as arranged, sitting on the stairs to the club. I could feel my heart beginning to pound, my hands sweating. I was about to go to senior police and turn in a whole detectives' office. *Who in hell did I think I was?* I didn't want to be a 'dog', just a detective without the prospect of becoming a prison inmate.

Kim looking very bloody serious didn't help. "Don't worry, you'll be all right," he said.

We walked up the internal stairs of the building after being let in via an intercom. Detective Chief Superintendent Robert Myatt opened an internal door to us. Kim knew him and introduced me. We went up some more stairs to a small cheerless office in the drab concrete building. Kim introduced me to Chief Superintendent Mervyn Schloeffel and Superintendent Robert Myers. As he was the boss, Schloeffel was behind a large wooden desk. He had an unusual-shaped head without much hair, and beady eyes. Myers had a touch of style about him and sat to the side of the desk. I was offered a seat.

"Well, I must be going now," announced Kim, seconds before walking out the door. I had thought he was going to stay with me through the interview. But the door closed and he was gone.

I now had the undivided attention of two very serious-looking men. Here I was, a twenty-four-year-old policewoman, about to tell the head of Police Security that their Police Force stank.

Schloeffel spoke first, in a professional voice. "Well, I believe you have some information for us about Parramatta?"

So I started. They instantly knew what restaurant I was referring to when I described the big lunch party. They also knew who the two flashy used car salesmen were who had been at the lunch; they were known as high-level drug dealers. They had also heard of Danny. I told them that during the lunch I had used the mobile phone of one of the used car salesmen, calling Irene to tell her I would not be home for dinner as I was still at lunch with the boys. "Why don't you trace the mobile phone call coming into my parents' house to tie it in?" I suggested to Schloeffel.

"We can't trace incoming phone calls." I knew from talking to the Telecom boys that this was not correct.

I wouldn't have come to them if I hadn't been so scared. I admitted to them that it was getting my fingerprints on the gun licence for Lennie McPherson's wife that had made me contact Cook. They both just sat there listening to me with perplexed expressions. I didn't know what to think. Schloeffel gave me the impression he wanted me to stop talking. He just didn't seem interested. He then started asking me questions about a uniformed officer in Parramatta, someone who wasn't even in the detectives' office.

As we spoke it dawned on me that no one appeared to be making a record of my complaints. Schloeffel informed me that the restaurant where we had had the lunch with Roger Rogerson was an old gaming premises. He said the used car salesmen were recruiting new crims just out of gaol, and the lunch must have been celebrating a major jewellery store robbery that they were aware of. I remembered all the flashy gold and diamond rings. But Schloeffel kept going back to the uniformed officer. It was as if he had a personal vendetta against him.

It was now the end of our conversation. "Get us a copy of the CIR [Criminal Information Report] from the break and enter you filled out," suggested Schloeffel. "Leave the matter with us."

Thinking back I find that to be a very strange thing to ask. The report was completed in triplicate and a copy was held at the Central Index Unit for storage. Why would he ask me to go into a busy detectives' office to get a copy and risk blowing the whole case? Such an act could place me in great physical danger. If some of these guys saw I was even aware of the document, I would be in serious trouble – they didn't muck around.

Later that week, sitting at my desk back at the office, I was nervously waiting for the right time to get a copy of the break and enter report. "What are you doing, Debbie?" quipped Lloyd. "Are you going to try and get a copy of your report?"

I thought, *Did he just say what I think he said?* I decided that I was being paranoid, getting spooked because I was so scared. Yet later in the shift Lloyd and Detective Sergeant Mark Brady both told me that the office had a source at IPSU. They had been told I had supplied information about the office.

Less than a week after I went to IPSU, people at Parramatta knew about it. The leak had certainly placed my life at risk. People became distant, gave me antagonistic looks and ignored me.

Whitey came out of his office, which was a rare occurrence, and walked from desk to desk warning everyone not to say anything on the phone. "IPSU has tapped the phones. No one is to say anything incriminating on the telephones."

He glared at me as he walked past. This frightened me and made me very uncomfortable. Another colleague made it very obvious he knew. "Gee, the phones are hot now," he said, coming up to my desk. "You've done a silly thing, Debbie; you're a silly little girl."

I was horrified, my face burning bright red. Unable to speak I thought, *How could this happen?* I needed to go back to the source.

On 24 April I rang Schloeffel and told him, "There's been a leak. People at Parramatta know that I have made a complaint. It's getting very nasty for me out here."

"Okay, just take it easy. Tell me what's happened."

"I'm scared. Grigg knew I was trying to get a copy of the Crime Incident Report you asked me to get for you."

"Don't jump to any conclusions. You've got nothing to worry about."

"They told me they have an informant in your office, and that the phones are hot."

After what seemed like a considerable pause, Schloeffel spoke, "We'll transfer you to the Commissioner's Policy Unit at Police Headquarters. Report there on 26 April at 7am."

The Commissioner's Policy Unit took up a whole floor of Police Headquarters opposite Hyde Park. I think it was on the seventeenth or eighteenth floor. The commissioner's office was on the top floor, the twentieth. When the lift doors opened, Superintendent Col Cole was standing there. He was a large, overweight officer with short dark hair. In full uniform and with a serious look on his face, he was a bit intimidating. He escorted me around to a desk that was not in an office, but in an open floor space. After I was seated he went off somewhere while I waited, feeling partly numb. Upon his return he leaned over close to me. "We don't want to bother Mr Avery the Commissioner with all this," he said quietly. "He's about to go. But Mr Lauer [then Assistant Commissioner Tony Lauer, Head of Professional Responsibility] is going to be the next commissioner so he may as well deal with it. I'll go and get him. He'll come back and talk to you."

He then left again. His words have stayed in my mind because at that time I hadn't heard that Lauer was going to be the next commissioner. I didn't know Avery was going, for that matter. I remained seated at the desk, scanning the office. A flash of something green struggling to grow in a plastic tub occasionally disturbed the wall panels made of brown imitation timber laminate. Being transferred out of Parramatta virtually overnight, I'd never been up to the executive levels in Police Headquarters before and I didn't know what was going to happen to me. As a lowly constable, the thought of speaking to the next commissioner was awesome.

Time crept by slowly while I was left sitting at the desk. Questions begged for answers. How could a leak have happened from IPSU? They were the special Internal Affairs. The elite. How could this have happened to me?

Col Cole finally came back and introduced me to Assistant Commissioner Tony Lauer. He then scurried off again.

Mr Lauer, whom I had never seen before, was a tall man of medium build, and wearing uniform. What struck me most was the way his bottom lip drooped down, as if it had an aversion to the rest of his face. He had short, greying hair that appeared to be highlighted with hair tonic. He sat down opposite me and started talking. "I know about your situation," he began. "What's happened?"

I started to tell him that people at the Parramatta Detectives' office knew what had happened and were very angry with me for speaking to IPSU.

"What are we going to do with you?" he asked. "Where do you live?"

"I live at Glenorie with my parents."

"We can't put you anywhere out there because Parramatta is the head station to all that area, there's no point in us putting you near those people. Where would you like to go?" he asked. "What would you like to do?"

I was bewildered, thinking, *Well, where is there to go? Where do I go now? What happens to me?*

I started rambling, as I tended to do when nervous. I told him what was happening at Parramatta detectives, including the lunch with Rogerson and Bayeh, and what I knew of Ron's activities.

"There's serious stuff going on," I told him.

Lauer said they were looking into it. "The main thing today is, what are we going to do with you?"

Feeling that I hadn't convinced him how serious the corruption was out there, I kept attempting to tell him more.

"Police don't like whistleblowers," he stated.

I had never heard the term, 'whistleblower' before. I didn't know what he meant, but it didn't sound good. "What's a whistleblower?" I asked.

"Police who dob in other police."

By the end of the conversation there was no doubt in my mind that Lauer knew not only that I'd spoken to IPSU, but what I had told them.

I was almost begging, pleading for help. This was the upcoming Police Commissioner: there was nowhere else to go. His body language, his face and his tone of voice made me think it was I who was at fault by speaking out.

I felt like a silly little girl who had done something that everyone else knew not to do. There was apparently an unwritten rule that everyone else knew, except me. It was to be many years before I learned that the term 'whistleblower' meant any employee who reported corruption or malpractice. I thought it was a term from days when police carried whistles.

It really hit me that I was making a fool of myself in front of the next commissioner, so I started to back off a bit

"We will put you with Michael Drury," said Lauer. "You're both outcasts."

If Lauer was telling me that I was in the same boat as Drury, I had better start paddling fast.

Col Cole returned and I was taken to an office on the same floor. After what seemed a long time, Michael Drury appeared and I was introduced to him. Drury didn't look impressed about being stuck with me. I don't know what they had told him about me, but maybe he just didn't want a sidekick.

I went home and told Irene that I had been put with Drury. She started yelling hysterically. Both she and John were very worried for their little girl. "They put you with bloody Drury because they are going to shoot you next," said Irene, not comforting me at all. "I can't believe you could be so stupid. What were you thinking?"

Every night the three of us would close the curtains and sit in the lounge room, watching television and waiting for something to happen. It was a depressing, soul-destroying situation. I started to sit and drink with them and a real depression began to set in. Did I have a future? All seemed hopeless. Losing contact with all my friends, I wasn't only isolated at work but also socially. This was the darkest period of my life, when my drinking slipped from a few social glasses with the boys into a lonely escape within the bottle.

Sitting on the lounge with John, I would roll his cigarettes for him and we would watch television together. This was not how a twenty-five-year-old girl should have to be spending Friday and Saturday nights. My lust for life was diminishing and comfort eating was causing the weight to creep on. Life felt like it was going down the drain. The career I had cherished so dearly was on the scrapheap waiting for "them" (the bad guys, police and crooks) to get me.

CHAPTER 11

OPERATIONS WAVE AND WINDMILL

I started working at Task Force Wave on 26 April 1988 and spent approximately two years there with Detective Sergeant Michael Drury in charge. To start with, there were just the two of us. Every cop in New South Wales knew the name Michael Drury; being shot that night in 1984 had made him a legend.

Mick and I would join up at predesignated times in coffee shops and touch base. I rarely ventured into his office in Police Headquarters; I worked from the old CIB building in Campbell Street, Surry Hills. It was originally an old hat factory before the police bought it and now it was 90 per cent unoccupied. There was, however, a security guard on the front door. It was a desolate old building and especially creepy at night. There were a couple of task forces working on the other floors as well as an intelligence gathering group.

There was also the Blackburn investigation. Harry Blackburn was a retired police superintendent charged with a number of sexual assaults. He was vigorously pursued by investigators, even though some forensic evidence excluded his involvement in the crimes. The arrest caused a great deal of publicity, with Harry being marched past the media outside Police Headquarters at the time of his arrest. Charges were withdrawn, but there was reason to conduct a Royal Commission into the handling of the investigation. Many senior police were criticised for their involvement in the investigation, including Tony Lauer. However, the only police officer charged in relation to the conduct of the investigation was the most junior constable. Blackburn received almost $1 million in compensation.

The noisy old lift would slowly move between floors, taking forever to get to our office on the third. It was so old you had to manually close the large heavy door. My cold and lonely glass office had a single timber desk and filing cabinet. Each passing hour seemed like four. Being deprived of social contact increased my loneliness and depression: I was swallowed up by a black pit of despair.

Being in Michael's presence was a comfort. He understood the loss and the grieving I was going through. Yet he was a smoker, and I couldn't stand the air being continually full of cigarette smoke. It was bad enough with John at home and his roll-your-owns. Mick took pity on a dumb kid who had found herself out of her depth. He gradually warmed to me and became a friend and confidant. He told me that when he thought he was dying he said Roger Rogerson had been involved in his shooting, but because he survived, his statement never stood up. He also told me that he gave evidence in

Rogerson's trial, but the Dodger ended up being acquitted. Mick explained that at one stage, when things were hot, his whole family had been sent to the USA for a period. It seemed to me that he had been badly affected by his experiences. How could you ever be the same after staring death in the face?

This Task Force Wave, targeting car thieves, was one of the best-kept secrets I've seen for the waste of taxpayer's money. The time was late 1988 and Ted Pickering was the New South Wales Minister for Police. He had a reputation as a bit of a cowboy. Rumour was that lights and a siren were attached to his ministerial car – the 'I want to be a policeman when I grow up' syndrome.

Anyway, I had entered the waiting zone with Michael and six old cars that were going to change the face of car theft control. We had an old beige Kingswood, and then there was an old red Ford, with a paint job washed out from years of neglect. The prize of the fleet was an old white Datsun with windscreen wipers that didn't work. And I haven't even mentioned the Commodores with their ripped upholstery. These six vehicles were so clapped-out that no self-respecting car thief would ever consider stealing them, nor would any pimply-faced teenager wanting a joy ride. At any given time at least one car would be off the road.

These rust buckets were known as the 'Gotcha' cars. A fortune was spent setting them up with alarms and sirens. When someone tried to break into a car, metal bolts would shut and the thief was supposed to be trapped inside. Mr Pickering was so revved up over his little baby he wanted a sign to pop up from the dash saying, "Stop, the police are on the way." He also wanted a recorded voice activated to say, "You have been trapped by the Gotcha police cars. Stay still until the police arrive." The ultimate request was for gas to fill the car to prevent thieves from escaping. Michael pointed out to a senior officer that if someone had an asthma attack and died, Pickering could be held liable. That idea was soon scrapped.

"It's ridiculous! They are spending hundreds of thousands of dollars on the system, yet using absolutely worthless cars," I kept arguing with Michael. Then there was, of course, all the money spent on wages for the police involved in the operation. It didn't make sense. I argued that the resources should be turned around. Surely using two good cars with anti-theft systems would be more productive. All my comments fell on deaf ears.

The cars were kept in the locked yard at the rear of the hat factory. A short time later five constables, one from each police region, were brought in to work on the task force. They were all still on probation; I was told this was because it would be good work experience for them and none of the crooks would know their faces. It seemed a bit strange, but someone probably received a promotion for it. We would have a car each, and we got to take them home, although they were very unreliable.

I was made second-in-charge of the task force, Michael's helper. "I'm very busy writing my book at the moment," he told me. "There's even talk of a movie." Michael was writing *In the Line of Fire* with Darren Goodsir. I had coffee with them once. Michael was big on sitting in coffee shops and drinking endless cups of coffee while enjoying a cigarette. I think his biggest defect of character is that he was just *too* nice a bloke to be in the force. In fact he is a gentleman, a rarity these days, in the police or anywhere else.

"I need you to run things out on the road for me," he told me. "I also have other duties and the surveillance course to run. Keep me up to date and I will sign all the meal claims." I just looked at him dumbfounded; not only did I have no management experience, but I was barely functioning. A Detective Constable First Class, I now had the responsibility of running a ministerial task force with five pimply-faced woodchucks looking to me as their leader. I just wasn't up to it.

I gave it my best shot, of course. Each morning I would pick what looked like a major shopping centre and we would head off to park our cars. After setting up we would wait for our beepers, which looked more like remote controls for roller doors, to go. As the day went on the boredom would set in. It was brain-numbing work, but beggars can't be choosers.

We would park the vehicles in shopping centres or railway car parks, but no one would touch them. In the end we were so desperate we left them unlocked with money and purses visible on the seats. Even this didn't work; a couple of times good Samaritans notified the police or local security officers about an unlocked car with a purse in it. In fact, nobody was ever arrested the whole time I was at the task force. I know for a fact the Gotcha cars never caught a car thief.

It was boring, lonely work. Every three months I was given a new set of woodchucks, one from each of the five regions. These five, plus myself, made up the crew for the six Gotcha cars. I don't even remember most of their names or faces. And while I was trying to cope with pain in my chest from the constant fear of waiting for something dreadful to happen, my drinking really took off. But I had nowhere else to go while I waited for the bomb that was Parramatta to blow up. The thought of running into officers from Parramatta haunted my thoughts. Every morning I waited for the newspaper headline about Parramatta, or in the evening a news flash interrupting *The Brady Bunch.*

It was confusing to think that I had done something really wrong by speaking out about what was happening at Parramatta. I was now being punished by being stuck out there in the twilight zone. I felt very ashamed, believing my career was ruined.

In April 1989, following the information I supplied to Schloeffel at IPSU, Operation Windmill was established by Internal Affairs to investigate Parramatta Detectives' office. A few months after my first interview at Regent Street I was called in to look at some surveillance photographs taken of the police coming and going from the Parramatta office. They now wanted me to identify the faces.

After a while I began to wonder what in the hell I was doing there. They couldn't seriously need me to identify other police from the Parramatta office. And all the crooks were better known than even the police were. There wasn't anyone in the photographs they did not already know. After about an hour they sent me on my way. They didn't ask me to make a statement or take part in a record of interview. Apart from coming in on this occasion, I never heard from Schloeffel or anyone else in Internal Security about the investigation.

I nearly fell over when I realised that Lloyd Grigg from Parramatta went to IPSU with additional information concerning corruption at Parramatta Detectives. Something must really have scared him to go to the lengths I had. He was subsequently placed at Operation Wave in the hat factory under the protection of Michael Drury, taking my old position a short time after I left. I felt sorry for him. Constables Fagan and Anderson from the Anti-Theft Squad at Parramatta also made complaints.

So two detectives had separately reported corruption on a major scale. Yet at the Royal Commission that was eventually set up, when senior investigators from Internal Affairs were questioned about the identity of the male detective who came forward with information no one remembered who he had been. He had been transferred to the old hat factory, as I had and Blind Freddy could have worked out who he was.

Detective Inspector Wayne Chapman, who worked under Detective Superintendent Bob Myatt at IPSU around this time, said it was not unusual for Myatt to send internal investigators out to a patrol to 'show the flag'. This was the practice of intentionally letting yourself be seen by detectives suspected of corruption to let them know that their activities were coming under notice. In other words, they were 'running too hot'. The intention was to get them to quiet down so that IA didn't have to take it any further. This usually had the desired effect.

On several occasions I went to the office of Chief Superintendent Col Cole on the top floor of Police Headquarters in relation to Operation Wave. It was a long trip up to the twentieth floor, a journey that not many police have travelled. When Mick Drury was away at the Goulburn Police Academy running the surveillance course, I would be on my own. He also took annual leave during the period I was in the hat factory. It was at these times I needed Cole's signature. Every day we were entitled to a meal allowance as we could not go to a police station for a meal. I lived on McDonalds during my stint in the factory.

One morning, I had just parked the Gotcha car in the car park at the rear of the hat factory. To get to the front doors of the factory I had to walk past the pub we had nicknamed the Jam Tin because of the small bar area and the need to stand shoulder to shoulder when more than a few patrons were there. I glanced down at my hands and noticed that they were shaking. I didn't make the connection between this and the fact that I was longing for the Jam Tin to be open, even though it was only seven in the morning. The thought of making the long trip up in the lonely lift to that little glass office with all the empty ones around it simply gave me the creeps.

I felt as if I was dying while I was hiding out. The fear and shame were soul-destroying and it was a case of get out or go under. The experience *was* killing me. Losing touch with reality, I just stopped caring. I wasn't wearing shoes at work any more and wandered around in old crumpled clothes. My justification was being undercover but sadly, it was more than that. I was in a very bad mental state but no one helped me. At no time did I receive any counselling or support. Not only that, but I was supposed to be running a badly planned, underresourced task force with inexperienced surveillance officers, as well as doing all the paperwork.

Things were not so great with Irene and John, either. On the day Michael Drury came out to Glenorie for lunch, he was shocked at the state of my parents as they greeted him. Active alcoholics on the path to oblivion, Irene and John were becoming a very serious problem. They no longer bothered with the little personal hygiene they'd once indulged in, such as washing their false teeth under a running tap or occasionally bathing or changing their clothes. At least Michael was spared the district nurse dressing the ulcers on John's legs that never seemed to heal. John had had several skin grafts, but they never seemed to take, mainly due to his poor circulation from years of smoking and drinking.

Trying to make an effort, I lit the BBQ out in the paddock to the side of the house. Around it were a number of rabbit traps welded open and painted white. Irene had done this as a bit of a joke as an uncle had once set signs along the road to his orange orchard stating, 'Beware man traps set'. The council had made him take them down.

Things tended to happen at our family barbeques. On one memorable occasion at about this time, Uncle Bill, who lived on the neighbouring property, staggered over to the BBQ after smelling the sausages and onions. Of course it was probably more likely the array of bottles on the table that enticed him. He was already as nearly drunk as we were. As he sat down I passed him a plastic cup of Malibu. Within an hour we were fully tanked and getting out of control. Being a big bloke who had gone to the war, Bill was as tough as nails.

A lot of history had gone on between his family and ours. I sidled up to Bill and looked him in the eye. "Where's the 1930 penny you took off my dead grandfather's body?" I asked. The next thing I knew, I was seeing stars after receiving four fast sharp punches to the jaw. Bill had a history of assaulting women. He was pretty brave when it came to hitting females.

When I was able to focus again I saw Bill running back to the safety of his side of the fence with Irene in hot pursuit. One thing you had to admire about Irene, she would rather have a fight than a feed, which was saying something considering the size of her. By the time I caught up to them they were near the BBQ in the middle of the paddock, swinging punches. Bill took his belt off, wrapping one end around his wrist, swinging the buckle end at us.

The whole time John sat on his seat with his head bowed. He was frightened of all three of us and he wasn't going to get involved. As far as I was concerned he was a mongrel who'd never stood up for Irene or me. I had no respect for John or Bill, they were both bad in their own ways.

With the advantage of his leather belt, Bill was getting the better of us. Irene, always the inventive one, realised that Bill was crook on his feet, so she took a chance. This little round ball of anger put her head down and charged. Luckily for her he collapsed on the ground. Irene then picked up a piece of wood from behind the BBQ and went to work on him. "This is the best day of my life," she yelled. "Die, you bastard!" Bill finally rose to his knees, but Irene managed to get in a few more kicks for good measure before he was up and running. The trophies for the day were the leather belt and a terry-towelling hat.

Within the hour we had an ambulance out the front of the house. I had a sinking feeling in my guts, and then two bosses from Parramatta turned up. They were angry and had rushed out to cause me some grief. This was all I needed. Irene had blood all over her. She stood up to the senior police and looked them in the eye, saying, "I did it all, look at the size of him and the size of me. I am a grandmother – do you want to arrest me?"

"Get in the ambulance," I told her.

"No fucking way, you have got to be kidding. I'll vomit going through the Galston Gorge in the back of a bloody ambulance." I was insistent and she eventually agreed. Upon arrival at the hospital they washed her down but couldn't find any injuries. "Oh, he hit me in the mouth and the blood was smeared on me from that," she said. I walked into the hospital's emergency section to get her with my head down; you could tell from the faces of the staff they knew it was someone else's blood. Mine. My jaw was black for weeks. I'm lucky Uncle Bill didn't break it, having been a boxer at one stage.

In the following weeks a member of the family kindly paid for a barrister to help my uncle sue me. The matter was eventually set down for Parramatta court. I could have cut my wrists. I wandered in and sat down in the waiting room for court to start, along with all the other idiots. I had dressed Irene and John in their best and they sat with me. A mate with whom I had gone through the academy was now a barrister, and he was kind enough to represent me for the price of a lunch.

We waited till ten o'clock. All the cops from the police station wandered up to laugh at me. They would walk past slowly and smirk as I waited for who knows what in the courtroom. At ten o'clock we were informed by Uncle Bill's solicitor that my uncle was too bloody scared to come to court and take me on. He had seen Irene and me in action in the paddock and he did not want to piss us off any further. Even though he was being pushed by my bastard relative to try and cause more grief, he was not that bloody stupid. So the case was thrown out.

These events had been utterly humiliating. I now felt I had no future, nothing to look forward to. I would just sit on the lounge and drink gin and cry about my sad life until I fell asleep and had some relief from the nightmare. To black out was like being dead and that was the only peace I had.

In July 1989, while I was up at Charles Sturt University in Bathurst doing residential study, a young fellow student talked me into going to a bachelor and spinsters' ball. The amount of alcohol I consumed that night nearly cost me my life. A couple of days later I was at the hat factory when the whole room started spinning. After a schnitzel with cheese for lunch, I returned to the office, whereupon the whole meal returned on me. I ran, but could only manage the male toilets, and then only the urinal.

Unable to move, I lay on the floor of the office the whole night. I hope never to be that sick again in this lifetime. The room kept spinning, preventing me from standing up. No security guard came up during the night to check the floor, so there I was on my own.

The next day Michael dropped in and I told him what had happened. He tried to tell me I'd had too much to drink, but I knew that wasn't the case as the dance had been three days earlier. This was something different, and it wasn't good.

Feeling green around the gills I soldiered on. Having this blind inbred stupid attitude that it doesn't matter how sick you are, you just get up and keep going, I didn't realise that my period was two weeks overdue. Now I was experiencing severe pains and slight bleeding. I knew something was not right and prayed that my one-night stand at the ball hadn't made me pregnant. (Not that I was religious then.)

The chemist was the next stop, to pick up a home pregnancy kit. It confirmed my worst fears. Continuing to bleed and with ever-increasing pain, I thought I was having a miscarriage, so I went for a curette. It made no difference. A week later and with the same symptoms, I returned to the clinic.

It was Friday afternoon and the doctor in charge wanted to go home. "What do you do for a living?" she inquired.

"I am a policewoman. I work on stolen cars."

Her expression darkened. "I had a Volkswagen," she explained. "The stupid police never found it. I loved that car."

I don't know whether she was holding me personally responsible, but she put me through hell. You wouldn't treat a dog the way she treated me. Her offsider looked on in horror. The doctor told me that because she had found nothing in my womb, I had no need to take the antibiotics she handed me. I knew that was bullshit because she had examined me thoroughly, trying to find the cause of bleeding. Eventually she said, "Go home. You don't need to stay. There is nothing wrong with you." When I later made a complaint about her attitude, she of course denied everything.

I knew something was terribly wrong as I lay curled up in bed. A few days later the bleeding and pain became worse and I drove myself over to the emergency department at Hornsby hospital. The sister recognised me from the times I had brought my parents in for treatment. She was unsympathetic and I was told they could not help. Days later I mustered the strength to attend Paddington women's hospital. Admitted overnight, I was given a D&C. A lovely Scottish doctor attended to my needs and was very kind. He informed me that he could not find anything in the uterus and the next day I was sent home.

By the next week I was haemorrhaging and passing out from the pain. Curled up in bed in the foetal position, I pulled the sheets over my head and could feel myself slipping away. Suddenly I had to decide if I was going to live or die. Pulling together all my energy I reached out to the phone beside the bed to ring Paddington women's hospital again.

Miraculously the nice Scottish doctor answered the phone. "It must be an ectopic," he deduced, clearly concerned. "Get in here now, I'll tell them you're coming."

I climbed into one of the old Gotcha cars and began the hour-long drive into Paddington. I don't know how I completed the journey. If I had passed out from the pain while I was driving, I might have killed other people on the road. I was so ill that I just wasn't thinking straight.

When I arrived at the hospital they took a blood test. I *was* still pregnant. "You will be going into surgery in fifteen minutes," said one of the nurses. "Go to the toilet and make a telephone call to tell someone what is happening."

At last, some urgency about my condition. I rang Irene to tell her I was going into theatre. I was very upset, having never been in hospital for myself before. "Hurry up and get down here," I pleaded.

The next thought was to ring Michael on his mobile. He arrived at the hospital before I went into the theatre. He was very kind and organised for the work car to go back to the yard.

Before I went into surgery I bumped into Chantal, the working girl I had met in Kings Cross when I first started. She also remained to give comfort until they wheeled me in.

I had never previously believed in God, having joked that when I was about to die, I would change my mind just to cover my bases. But now that the chips were down, I was not joking. In the toilet cubicle I said my first prayer, promising God that if He let me live, I would lead a more productive and worthwhile life. I didn't realise at the time that the promise I was making was to give up drinking.

After the operation, regaining consciousness for brief moments while on the morphine drip and with tubes coming out of my stomach, I kept asking for my parents. The nurses looked embarrassed. They hadn't come to the hospital. I couldn't believe it; for the first time in my life I really needed them, and they were not there. Their reaction to the news of my condition was to get really pissed. The next day they were too crook to attempt the trip to the hospital. It was three days before they came to see me.

I discovered that one of my fallopian tubes had burst, that I had been bleeding into my gut and my stomach was infected. That lonely hospital bed was my home for a whole month. After about three weeks I woke one afternoon to find my brother visiting me for the first time. He was sitting by the bed reading my newspaper.

"What are you doing here?" I asked.

"Tell your mother to stop ringing me and asking me to visit you."

Unable to comprehend his attitude, I rallied the strength to abuse him, which resulted in him scurrying off with a look of annoyance. As the saying goes, you can pick your friends but not your relatives.

Noticing the lady in the next bed was crying one day I became concerned for her. Why was she was so upset? Apparently the cause was my many phone conversations with my drunken mother, who kept calling to inform me that I was a selfish bitch and I should sign myself out and come home and look after her and John. I kept hanging up on her, but my poor neighbour was finding it all very distressing. At the time I was unable to understand why: this was normal for me and what I expected from my family. I had copped so much abuse from my biological family and my police family that I had no sense of what was appropriate.

It was a long month, and I had time out for me. Time to reflect on life and look at where I was going. Making a pact with God, I decided to live and not just exist for the benefit solely of others. Not drinking made my mind clearer. On the three occasions Irene and John visited they abused me, telling me how hard it was for them to make the trip in and how the walking had caused more ulcers on John's foot. They could have driven in, of course, but they were always over the limit. On the other hand, they would not get a taxi as that was a waste of good drinking money. Helping themselves to my Visa card on the second visit, they replenished their alcohol supply. On their third visit, they left two cans of UDL vodka and passionfruit. Now I can see how sad that is.

When I was ready to leave, Irene wouldn't drive in to bring me home from hospital, so I caught a taxi to Glenorie wearing my nightie, which was very embarrassing. Leaving the hospital at two in the afternoon was just another humiliation to endure. Not to mention arriving home to encounter John and Irene smashed on the verandah. God, how I hated my life.

Back at the hat factory I found myself walking into Michael's office. Enjoying a morning coffee, he was looking at some paperwork between glances at the morning's newspaper.

"I'm leaving the task force to go back to mainstream policing," I said.

"What's brought this on?"

"This is killing me, being in hiding. I think I need to move on."

"Are you sure this is what you want? Where do you want to go?"

"I don't know. To one of the squads maybe. I'll make some phone calls. If I don't go soon I may never get out."

I completed the detective's course successfully in March 1990, and by May I had my sights on a fresh start. Michael Drury wasn't happy about my going, but he understood I wanted out. Somewhere smart where I could wear a suit and clean up my act. Desperate to get out of Operation Wave, I thought somewhere like the Fraud Squad would allow me to put my appalling experiences behind me. Anticipating that life in the Fraud Squad would consist mainly of paperwork, I would avoid exposure to corrupt detectives.

CHAPTER 12

LIFE IN THE FRAUD SQUAD

It was starting to dawn to me that no big raid on the Parramatta Detectives' office was imminent. I had thought, naively, that those in charge would want to know about serious corruption at one of the state's most significant detectives' offices. But I suspect that, while they probably knew the extent of the problem, attempting to tackle it would cause dire political ramifications. I still believed I had done something wrong and had committed the ultimate crime: betraying my workmates.

Detectives, it seemed, were above the law, a phrase that later became the title of a short-lived police drama TV series. (One of the main characters was Debbie the policewoman. Talk about art imitating life. The actor who played Debbie is a friend of mine, a beautiful young girl on her own amazing journey, moving on to better roles. This lovely girl was even at one stage our babysitter.)

Having made up my mind to transfer to the Fraud Squad, I needed to figure out how. With the hide of Ned Kelly I phoned the office and spoke to a man with a wonderful foreign accent: Detective Senior Sergeant Aldo Lorenzutta, who was relieving the commander and was a bit of a rough diamond. He invited me down to the Fraud Squad office in the Remington building opposite Hyde Park. As we drank coffee and chatted, I looked over a large open-plan office with great views of the park and the north of the city. A number of smart-looking gentlemen wearing business shirts with ties were talking on phones and typing at computers.

The squad had about forty officers, including one woman: Claudia Campanelli, an Italian girl about whom I had heard many rumours. Apparently she was on annual leave that day and so I was to miss meeting her again.

Aldo gave me a warm welcome, saying he felt they needed a touch more femininity in the office. I should have recognised this as a sign. I went back to the twilight zone office and rang Michael. He was very unimpressed that I had followed through on my decision to leave, but agreed to speak to Aldo, whom he knew from around the traps. Remain a detective long enough and you get to drink or work with most of them at some stage.

The following week I had coffee with Michael. "I've seen Aldo," he reassured me. "Everything is okay for you to start on Monday morning." The Fraud Squad kept regular office hours of 8am to 4.30pm, Monday to Friday, as they dealt mainly with white-collar crime among large financial institutions.

When I told Irene and John about my new job, they freaked

out. Why wouldn't I want things to stay as they were? Coming out of hiding made me an easy target. But I knew exactly why I didn't want things to stay as they were. I was twenty-five, living at home, doing all the housework, supporting three adults, four Maltese terriers, twelve chooks and a large Eastern Grey kangaroo named Elvis. (My cousin had borrowed him during a drunken prank and the kangaroo ended up on our doorstep the night 'the King' died.) Being the cunning creature that she was, and much to her dislike, Irene realised the gravy train was about to stop. *I* was about to get a life.

On Monday morning I travelled into town at about 6am, with Irene and John in tow. Why? I don't know. After breakfast in the city they were then given detailed instructions on how to get back home. As the three of us walked through Hyde Park a pigeon did what pigeons do right down the back of my shirt. "That's a good omen," Irene declared with mad gypsy eyes. "Things are going to change for you." How right she was.

As I walked into the Fraud Squad office, I noticed that Aldo's friendly face was absent. A weasel-like detective in a shiny grey suit slipped up to me, and said, "Jamo stabbed Aldo in the back."

Apparently Aldo and Detective Senior Sergeant Terry Jamison were to alternate relieving in the commander's position until it was filled. Jamo had decided not to share the chair. "So Aldo is out of here," said the detective. "He's not stupid, and you don't cross Jamo." The wind went out of me. With Aldo there had been hope of working with a real, breathing human being. Unfortunately in the cops, nice people tend to come last.

Jamison made it very clear that he did not want or need another woman. He already had one. Bloody Aldo had a hide to take on new staff while he was only relieving for him. I didn't point out that Aldo thought he had a fair chance of becoming the boss. Evidently the politics here were the same as elsewhere. "Since you are here, you can go out and assist Senior Sergeant Rome Martin," said Jamo.

Rome had obviously been a handsome man in his day. He was what you would refer to as a good style of a bloke, but prematurely wrinkled from too much time in the sun on weekends. While he gushed over me, his first request was to make him a coffee, no sugar.

Later that day we went for a drive around Watson's Bay. Rome must have thought I would find this romantic. When it became obvious that I wasn't interested in him, he became hostile. When we returned to the office I was reduced to coffee maker and typist; a designated Detective Constable First Class, I was now reduced to retyping his bloody statements. Rome had never entered the computer age, having failed the computer course twice and given up. He was still using an electric typewriter, one of only a few the Police Department still owned.

The other senior sergeant, whose desk also faced towards the rest of the investigators in the office (they were like the teachers at the front of the classroom), was George McTaggart. George never had a good word to say about anyone. He had been a grade footballer for Manly in his day, but now he was reduced to being a bitter old man, even if he did at least know how to turn on the computer. One of George's principal duties was completing Road Transport Authority (RTA) car registration checks for Nelson Chad, a former commander. During lunchtime it was mandatory to play six-handed cutthroat euchre if George so directed. I had played euchre with Irene and John when I was a kid, but never cutthroat. I was soon to become expert.

We also had a bar in the kitchen of the office, referred to as 'the mess'. At any one time the fridge held one out-of-date carton of milk, a cask of wine for the womenfolk and plenty of beer for the boys. Tooheys, of course. It was compulsory at 4pm to knock off, go into the kitchen, have a few and talk. The talk would comprise of telling old war stories about your greater arrests or taking the piss out of someone. Many a brain cell was destroyed in the old Fraud Squad mess.

One of the renowned customs of the section was Fraud Squad Friday. The office often organised a squad lunch to end the week and with any luck it would be paid for by a 'captain' (that is, a captain of industry, usually a representative of an insurance company or other financial institution). People who got too pissed at lunch often didn't bother coming back to work. Of course most of the senior officers had a police car to drive home, so they had some scrapes and dents to write off from time to time. One detective sergeant's car was known to all as 'the battered sav'. He finally drove the car through the front fence of a house two doors up from his home and was charged by one of the local police with 'refusal to undergo breath test'. This created quite a stir: not because he had destroyed a departmental vehicle, but because detective-sergeants aren't usually charged with drink driving offences.

"Bloody cockroaches, what's happening to the job?" people muttered.

In the mess one afternoon, a few of the senior detectives were filling me in on some of the characters in the office. "Never work with Greg Locke," I was warned. "If there's money to be found, he won't take any." I was surprised; he sounded like me, someone who went against what was expected because it was the right thing to do. He sounded interesting.

The next morning I had breakfast at Pancakes at the Rocks with about six guys from the office. Greg was one of the group and I was attracted to him from the start. He was over six foot tall, medium build, with short brown hair and an open, honest face. His courtesy and consideration were refreshing, but what first attracted me to him was his honesty. Maybe it was a silly thing to have as a come-on, but after all I had been through I was thrilled to find someone who thought as I did. While he was an outcast also, I wouldn't be sharing my secret with him for quite a while. I was ashamed at the mess my career was in and, after all, I had only received negative responses to what I had done about Parramatta. When I did begin letting Greg in on some of my experiences he was kind, supportive and allowed me to realise *I* had not done anything wrong. Yet it would be many years before I actually believed this.

About two weeks later I was introduced to Claudia, the only other woman at the squad. She was beautiful and slender with long wavy auburn hair, and in her elegant tailored suits she had a real presence about her. What was also remarkable about Claudia was that she was a real person — something that didn't help her. She was friendly, pleasant, warm and open-hearted. She showed me real kindness. As the only two women in the office, we quickly became very close.

The system in Fraud at that time was that each investigator worked with a senior officer to guide and train them in conducting major fraud investigations. There were approximately forty investigators at the section. I was allocated a partner for approximately three months out of the entire three years I was there. Despite numerous requests I was never placed with a permanent partner, even though the section had a lot of undesignated police without plain clothes experience who were junior to me. They did of course have the advantage. They were male.

As I walked out of the office one day about a week after arriving at the squad, Senior Sergeant George McTaggart slid up close to me in the hallway. "I know what you did at a Parramatta," he said in a menacing tone. "I know all about what you're at."

From that day on he treated me with contempt and hostility. Even though I was a skinny little blonde thing, he was constantly making comments to put me down. He would allude to my supposed heavy weight whenever he could, even though I was a size twelve. On several occasions he gave me magazine articles on grooming to read and once he gave me the *Fit for Life* book to copy on the police photocopying machine. He was nasty to me at any available opportunity, yet when he was later interviewed by Internal Affairs about his treatment of me he told them what good mates we were, and that we even exchanged recipes. This was not true.

On 27 August 1990 I went over to the Police Welfare Unit in Wentworth Street to speak to someone about the problems I was having at the Fraud Squad. (I ended up speaking to them on a number of occasions.) After waiting a while, I was pointed to the office of one of the psychologists.

"What can I do?" I asked after I explained the problems I was facing.

"Listen, I'll keep a record of the problems you're having. Come back in if you feel like you would like to talk further."

"Is that all you can suggest?" I was really dismayed.

"It's terrible what is happening to you. Why don't you think about moving to another section?"

"Why should I have to move? I've already had to transfer a couple of times to get away from harassment."

They didn't do anything to help me. On one occasion I was told that as I had managed to put lipstick on before seeing them, I could not be *that* stressed. I didn't even have the strength to tell them Claudia had applied it for me because I was in such a state. She was trying to make me look better that day before I saw them.

I could have taken my concerns to the Equal Employment Opportunities branch of the Police Department. My first experience with this department had been in 1985 while I was attached to North Sydney, as part of my secondary training at the Police Academy. After the head of the department gave a lecture on EEO issues he had invited anyone with problems to stay back and talk to him. Constable Rebecca Booth and I went to see him in the corridor, wanting to talk about the sexual harassment I was experiencing at the time from one of the constables at North Sydney.

"Listen, girls," he told us, "it's a man's job. If anyone harasses you, put up with it and keep it quiet. Otherwise your life will be a misery. If something detrimental is said about the officers involved, their careers would be tarnished. If you don't like it, just get out."

So I knew there was no point in going to him. In retrospect, while his advice might not have been appropriate, it was at least honest. But there was one bright spot on the horizon. Within about one month of beginning work at the section I began a personal relationship with Greg Locke. The relationship was frowned upon and we kept it quiet for as long as possible.

At about this point the cruel reality of my life truly sank in. I felt that if I died no one would care. This was not a cheerful thought and, if true, it meant that my life up until this point hadn't amounted to much. I was the strong one in the family, the rescuer, the one who sorted out legal and other hassles, the one who got sick alcoholics into hospital. At the age of twenty-five, I had the weight of the world on my shoulders. Coming from the family I did, I never had much of a childhood. Now that I was running the show, everything that went wrong was also my fault. As well as being the rescuer, I was the scapegoat. If the puppy had kittens it would be my fault.

Something wasn't right but I just couldn't put my finger on it. Perhaps I was destined to be one of those people who went through life from one crisis to another. But I also felt that life wasn't meant to be this bloody hard and awful. Irene had introduced me to other victims in Glenorie, people in their fifties and sixties who had given up their chance at happiness and stayed at home and looked after their parents. "You're my old age insurance policy," she told me. One day in a rare moment of clarity she looked at me with those watery light blue eyes. "What would have happened if I had never had you?"

Trying to find the strength to continue enduring life, I picked up the Yellow Pages. I think a higher power was at work, but whatever the cause I found the phone number for Centacare, a Catholic counselling organisation. This was even more miraculous because Irene had brought me up to distrust Catholics. She had gone to St Joan of Arc primary school at Haberfield, and her parents had planned for her to become a nun. "What a beautiful novice you're going to be," they would say, pulling her hair back. She had jumped through a window to get out of that one. I had been brought up on Catholic horror stories, yet the Catholics were the first people I ever turned to for help.

When I went for counselling sessions I didn't even know what my problems were. The kindness I was given was extraordinary and the woman there had the wisdom to steer me to the twelve-step fellowship of Alanon, the organisation set up to help the relatives of alcoholics. I remember my reluctance, telling her that if I went to a support group and spoke about Irene and John there would be repercussions at home. I argued that if I did leave my parents, who were slowly killing me, I knew them well enough to know they would probably kill themselves. Irene had brainwashed me from a young age with the concept that it was the three of us against the world. Convinced that I was born to look after them, I would also drink myself to death in the old farmhouse at Glenorie, as family tradition dictated.

For the next few months I kept seeing my counsellor. Greg attended a session with me. Encouraged by the concept of Alanon, he dragged me to my first meeting. After looking up the meeting list I made him come out to Glenorie to get me, then drive me to Mosman. We travelled a long way from home just in case I was seen going to a meeting about alcoholism. In retrospect it seems insane. But going to a meeting for the first time felt like stabbing my family in the back.

The cold wind circling the church hall was very confronting at 8pm. An odd group of people sat around in a circle and took turns at sharing. They had nothing in common except having to handle the disease of alcoholism. I couldn't believe people were talking about the same things we had kept secret for generations. I learned that when you tapped a watermelon and poured methylated spirits inside, it did not magically turn into watermelon wine. I learned that other people who looked normal and were well dressed had grown up in horrific circumstances similar to mine. Most importantly, they had survived and lived to tell the tale. I am forever grateful for their courage, strength and hope.

Trying to process so much information was so difficult as my whole life was based on a lie. The way we lived was *not* the Australian way of life, as Irene had insisted.

Greg dragged me back the next week. At this second meeting, the person putting out the chairs and coffee gave me the keys to the hall, saying, "I've changed jobs and can't open up any more. Why don't you do it for a while?"

"Er, I don't know . . ."

"Listen, don't worry, we can share the job."

Being landed with this service duty changed my life. Having an overbearing sense of responsibility, we were there every week at 8pm to open the door and set up. It never dawned on me that all the other people who were coming at five past eight could have opened up. Having to turn up every week, I slowly began to recover. I learned that alcoholism is a generational disease that not only kills the alcoholic but the others around them. Irene and John were sucking the life out of me. I was a young woman who had already lost my childhood but realised that I deserved a life. The right to a little happiness was mine, just as it was everyone else's right. At the same time I was falling madly in love with Greg. It didn't take me long to realise how different he was from all the other boyfriends I'd had in the past. Greg was kind, loving and very gentle.

I went to meetings every week for about six months, even starting to venture out to other groups. My life was changed again one night by an angel in the shape of a tiny old lady. After the meeting, where I had been sharing a particularly sad story and was justifying my sorrow and anger at being a victim, she came up to me and said, "Look, I'm sorry, but you're in the wrong room."

"Excuse me?"

"I've been around a long time and I know an alcoholic when I see one. You need to go across the hall to the Alcoholics Anonymous meetings. That is where you will really get well. You can't afford to drink at all, coming from the family you've come from."

"But *I* only drink to put up with the alcoholics in my life," I said. "They are sucking the life out of me. I can't cope any more."

This all of five foot tall grey-haired lady, who looked as if she would fall over if I blew on her, looked me straight in the eye and said, "You have to get recovery or you will die. Do you understand me? Half measures will do you absolutely no good at all. You have to go to any length to get recovery. You need abstinence to have a chance."

It wasn't just what she said, but how she said it. Somehow it slipped through the fog as she walked me across the corridor to where the alkies were. As painful as it was, I knew she was on the ball, I had to throw my hat in. I hated alcoholics; they had put me through so much pain. Feeling sorry for myself in Alanon had had its good side. Now I was about to declare to my parents that I was the enemy.

This was a real time of walking through fire. Greg would hold my hand and I would run into meetings after they had started, put my head down and sit up the back in case someone recognised me. I was so ashamed. Here I was, a twenty-five-year-old, attractive young woman who was a police officer. With years at university under my belt, I went on overseas trips, I had a car, I even ran a home. On the surface it looked as if I had my life together, yet I was going under.

It was suggested I attend ninety meetings in ninety days, and so my journey started. I would drive for hours to meetings all over the place and as soon as they were over I would run out the door in case someone tried to speak to me. Such was my fear. I did not want to think of myself as an alcoholic, yet on a subconscious level I must have known I was.

Grog was keeping me going; now I had to learn to perform without it. It was my god, my lover. Now I was being disloyal to it, wallowing in self-pity, moaning about not being able to go to an Italian restaurant any more if I couldn't enjoy a bottle of Lambrusca. I was disloyal to my parents. Irene would have killed herself if she knew what I was telling other people at meetings. Finding it difficult to function without alcohol, I'd been a workaholic all my life and always a bit on the manic side. Yet this has always been an asset as I'd been able to get so much done in a day. Now I was a shivering, shaking mess who didn't know which way was up; my nerves felt completely frayed. I was almost over a cliff, holding on to Greg by my fingernails; he was the only sure and stable thing in my life.

CHAPTER 13

MEETING THE PARENTS

It was a wet, cold winter's night and the 1990 World Cup soccer final was live on television. Greg wanted to watch it, but young romance was blossoming and it was time to meet the folks.

When we got to my place Irene and John were drunk, but at least they had their pyjamas on. The lounge room was thick with smoke, as John had been rolling Drum tobacco in his corner all day. He was deaf and practically blind and everyone had gotten into the habit of yelling at him. Irene was in the lounge room sitting in her favourite armchair. She made no attempt to get up.

"Would you like a beer?" she offered. "Or how about a port?" The flagon was positioned within reach.

"No, thank you," said Greg. "Maybe later."

The live soccer telecast was not until two in the morning. Having to work the next day we decided to set the alarm and take a nap, while John and Irene continued drinking in the lounge. They both kept their bottles in sight so the other didn't steal any. When it was time for the soccer, we returned to the party. "I've really been looking forward to this," said Greg. "Do you mind if I change the channel?"

"No of course not, go for it," said Irene. She hated sport with a passion but she knew she was well and truly out of her league with Greg. John kept talking away to himself.

I was excited to have Greg meet my parents. Despite my problems with them, on one level I was proud of how radical they were; whatever else, I had always thought they were really funny. Other friends from Glenorie thought they were cool too. They were always good for a drink and a yarn. We watched the game together that night, and when anything exciting happened, like someone scoring, Irene would jump up and dance in front of the television holding out the hem of her nightie. John and I thought this was very amusing, but I could see that Greg was not looking pleased.

"What's wrong with you?" I asked.

"I was really looking forward to watching the game."

"Yeah, but isn't she hilarious?"

"No. Can't you see there is something wrong here?"

John and Irene were turning blue in their cheap cotton nightwear, but they couldn't feel the cold. Greg looked puzzled. "I have to ask," he said to me. "Why are the front door, back door and side window open? I'm freezing."

"That is so you can run if someone comes at you with a knife," I explained. "We never shut any escape routes in this place."

"You have got to be joking." The blood drained from Greg's face. He had been brought up in a different world to mine. What I saw as normal he found disturbing.

"Why are you being so rude and not laughing at their jokes?"

"I'm sorry. I don't find them funny at all. Just sad."

The next day Irene rang me at work, as she usually did. "What do you think of Greg?" I asked.

"Piss him off. I don't like him. What's the go, Deb? He doesn't bloody drink. Does he think he is too good for us or what? I'm gonna call him the Wet Sock. That bloke won't last. You won't be able to stand him. He thinks he's too bloody good."

I continued seeing Greg and the romance flourished, much to Irene's displeasure. John was in his own little world and didn't care what was going on as long as he had some Drum tobacco and the next drink. Irene never offered Greg another drink, in her book the greatest insult anyone could inflict. On weekends I would have Greg mowing lawns and painting walls to a soundtrack of smartarse comments from Irene. He didn't seem to mind working outside; it meant less time with the folks.

What seriously worried Irene was her knowledge that Greg posed a real threat to her money supply and her lifestyle. With my having a real chance of happiness, all she was worrying about was her meal ticket. Irene would try to get a reaction out of Greg, either a laugh or make him lose his temper. But he would not bite, always maintaining a straight-faced expression. This was a skill he used to great effect at work as well as with family. His ability to not let others know what he was thinking drove my mother crazy.

At about this time, I had a lesson in what can happen to someone who lets his life be derailed. Graeme Adams and I had been mates from my early days at North Sydney. He was a year older than me and very tall. Graeme confided that his father had wanted him to be a professional tennis player and was greatly disappointed when his son chose a life in the cops. Apart from his height he had a certain stature that told you he had come from a good family with money. Quite the opposite background to mine.

Joining the Prosecuting Branch and studying law were further positive developments in Graeme's career. He was a likeable bloke and we often enjoyed a few drinks at the watering holes around the district. Our relationship was never sexual, we were just mates. As food and drink were also of huge interest to me, we had many big nights out. After a big session I was rarely interested in romance, let alone capable of it. Rather, I'd just drink more. Irene liked Graeme's sense of humour; it was black, like hers.

When I did see Graeme around the traps, we would stop and catch up. He was working as a prosecuting sergeant at the Downing Centre local courts in Liverpool Street in the city. To my surprise around 1989 he moved into a rented house at Galston, just a stone's throw from Glenorie. I suggested we travel into work each day together as it was such a long trip, and he gladly agreed.

His rented house was surrounded by bush and had a white wooden mailbox out the front. On the second day of travelling together I noticed that his mailbox had changed appearance. After he didn't come out when I tooted the horn, I went inside to hurry him up.

"Why's your letter box wrapped in aluminium foil?" I asked.

"So the locals know where to buy their drugs."

"You've got to be kidding!"

He made no reply except for a Cheshire cat grin.

My suspicion that Graeme had a drug addiction was confirmed, and I also noticed an aroma in the house that wasn't incense. He walked into his bedroom and came out a short time later with red bleary eyes. "I needed a line before I face court today," he explained. Even though I was a very heavy drinker, I was totally against drugs. A druggie is a much different creature to an alkie. He was definitely off his face, if our conversation into town was anything to go by.

After this trip I never picked him up again and made excuses why we couldn't travel together. I wasn't going to get into trouble because of someone else; I was supporting my family and job security was important. To cover myself I did mention this incident to a supervisor, but nothing ever came of it.

Graeme would go to the local RSL club, but would pretend he didn't know me. The locals didn't know he was a cop, which was probably better for business if he really was dealing drugs. A short time later I saw Graeme at the local shops. "We're having a big party at my place," he announced. "I've organised a pig on a spit."

"Sound's like it's going to be big."

"Yeah. We're even going to raffle off an ounce."

"Oh."

"You can't come, by the way," he informed me, looking serious. "I'm sorry, but I keep my private life very separate to my police life. Everyone out here knows you're a cop. Can't be seen with you. You'll give me a bad name."

A week later I heard though the local grapevine that the party had been raided by the police. Graeme later told me he escaped through the bush, but someone remembered a removalist van at the house and they were able to track down his flatmate who subsequently gave him up.

When I started to go out with Greg, I caught up with Graeme at a football match. "Can you do me a favour?" he asked.

"Yeah, what?"

"Do you mind asking Greg if he would care if you slept with both of us?" He had really lost the plot. He was not even asking me for a bonk, just for Greg's permission. It hurt me that he had so little respect for me and our friendship. After that stupid question I didn't bother catching up with him again. I couldn't believe my eyes when I saw the front page of the *Police News* a short time later. There he was, wearing a red clown's nose and that stupid grin of his. My immediate thought was, *Oh God, he's so stoned at work that he is wearing fancy dress in court.* But when I read the cover storey I saw that he was helping to support Red Nose Day for SIDS research.

One evening while Greg and some of his mates were having a beer, Grant Taylor mentioned Graeme Adams and Greg said he thought he was a druggie. Word got back to Graeme, who was angry enough to pass on a threat via Grant, which Greg ignored. When I saw Graeme in the street near the Downing Centre courts he just glared at me.

Graeme eased himself out of the Police Force not long afterwards. He ended up doing what a lot of suspect cops do when they have to get out of the job; he started up a private enquiry agency. His outfit was called Blue Falcon, a name that echoed his previous employment. On 6 June 2000 Graeme was seen walking on McMahon Street, Chatswood at 9.45pm with his business partner, and then he disappeared. At 8am on 12 July, more than a month later, police dragged his body out of the Hawkesbury River near Dangar Island. His legs and thighs had been wrapped in chains, his torso in garbage bags. He had been shot a number of times in the head, execution-style.

Graeme was a smartarse whose mouth could get him into a lot of trouble. He had been under investigation by detectives from the top-secret Operation Saigon in 1998. The following year, the Police Integrity Commission in public hearings named Blue Falcon, among others, as being under investigation for employing moonlighting police officers. The commission also detailed cocaine and ecstasy use and dealing by former and present police officers. Graeme's demise was as tragic as it was brutal. His story is another reminder of how people can lose their way when their involvement with illicit drugs gets out of their control. He had been a young man with so much promise – what a way to go, such a wasted life.

CHAPTER 14

TASK FORCE RORT

At the Fraud Squad I continued to work for further police qualifications. On 22 June 1990 I completed my Associate Diploma in Criminal Justice at Charles Sturt University. In September I completed the Commercial Crime course and finished a computer course in October.

I was always looking at ways to further my career, and repeatedly asked the boss if I could undertake the analyst course. This was a real desire of mine, as I really enjoy following the clues to get a result. But he always said no. Whenever a vacancy did come up he would send some other officer who was not even interested in this aspect of police investigation He could see how much it meant to me, but it seemed he was denying me the opportunity out of spite.

I walked into the Fraud Squad office one morning and George McTaggart greeted me with, "You're going to Wollongong!" Knowing the difficulties for my parents if I spent long periods of time away from home, I decided to ask Jamison if someone else could go in my place.

"Do I need to go to Wollongong?" I began. "I think there are plenty of other people who are keen to go."

"No, I want you down there."

"It's just going to create difficulties for me."

"You're not going to let your personal life interfere with your police career, Debbie?"

"If you are talking about Greg and me, it's got nothing to do with him. I have two very sick parents. They are completely dependent upon me. I have to do all the cooking and cleaning. The district nurse has to come in every day, they are that bad. They'll die if I have to work away from home."

But there was no budging him. He wanted me out of the office, it seemed, and yesterday.

So I travelled to Wollongong. After checking into the Royal hotel, the usual digs for big-city detectives on travel allowance, I headed into the office of Task Force Mort. It was situated in the main street of Wollongong, in a 1970s building that also housed a major insurance company. Our office was behind a glass partition at one end of the fourth floor, reached by a rickety, slow old lift.

I soon discovered why people in Sydney called this 'Task Force Rort.' Detective Sergeant Bill Gould, one of Jamison's favourites, was in charge of the investigation in Newcastle. He was a plump, ruddy-faced chap with little hair and unusually close-set eyes. When I walked into the office he was sitting on the desk chatting with Detective Senior Constable Bernie Foley, a younger man who also appeared to be having trouble keeping his hair, and whose carriage suggested he spent more time at the bar than the gym.

"Well, I'm here," I announced. "What's the go? What do you need done?"

"Hello, Debbie. Take it easy," Bill suggested. "There's no big hurry."

"Aren't you guys in a hurry to get back to that fraud brief? I thought you were getting near the end of that." This was a major fraud investigation that involved several million dollars. It had had teams of Fraud Squad detectives working on it for many months.

"Well, we'll put that on the shelf for now. What we're doing is staying down here on permanent travel allowance and when we get back from this, in a couple of years, we'll go and do all the round-the-world trips."

"What, and there are no problems with that?"

"No," said Bill with a wry smile.

One of my first duties on Mort was to accompany Bill and Bernie to the races for the day. This was the only time when I was invited along, although I know they went on many other occasions. They must have found me boring as I did not drink or gamble. And when they were on the prowl after a few beers, they also found me a bit of a handbrake.

We would go out and execute search warrants, seizing masses of documents that were then left in cardboard boxes on the office floor. The task force had no document control system of any kind. They were just collecting evidence about shonky, overpriced quotes given to a major insurance company, but weren't going to worry about organising it until later. As far as I could see they were constantly in party mode. I expressed my concerns to Bill a couple of times and eventually found a bookcase and put the boxes on the shelves to make the place look a bit tidier.

Being frustrated in my desire to do analyst work, I had found a former policewoman who had done the course and who very kindly showed me the basics. Not drinking left me with plenty of spare time on my hands, and I asked Bill whether I could handle the document control for the task force. Bill's response was, "Fine, good, go for it." So he basically let me become the analyst at Mort without being qualified.

I did my best to set up a system for document control. All task force documents were put onto charts, and all the briefs of evidence that had been completed were added. Each job was listed, with where they were up to and what work was outstanding. Bill knew that I'd been busy when I put the charts up on the wall behind my desk.

Serious drinking went on regularly during working hours. While I was staying at the Royal, where I was for a couple of weeks before renting a house in the suburbs, I had one serious relapse in my own drinking. I'd been thrown into turmoil, leaving John and Irene in Sydney. Not only that, but I had found the man of my dreams and I was packing up and leaving town. How could I keep the relationship with Greg going from such a distance?

On a weekend back in Sydney I went home to Glenorie. Irene looked at me with her bleary china-blue eyes. "How long are you going to be working on this job in Wollongong?"

"About two years."

"We won't last that long," she said, looking down through misty eyes. "We can't do this on our own."

Back in Wollongong we were all living in each other's pockets. I didn't even have the nous to find out where the meetings of Alcoholics Anonymous were; I was still embarrassed about my drinking problem. We were working ten days on and four off and I was silly enough to think I could go ten days without a meeting. Even after all these years I can't do that.

Not being a drinker caused a few social problems. "I don't trust people who don't drink," Bill Gould often reminded me. I got a very strong feeling that the last thing he had wanted in Wollongong was a bloody woman, let alone one who did not drink. I also got the feeling that he didn't trust me.

One night Bill returned from the bar with a big chocolaty-looking cocktail. "I'm your bloody boss," he said seriously. "And I'm directing you to drink this. I won't put up with this bullshit that you don't drink any more. I don't trust people who don't drink."

Defenceless, with him on my back all the time, I downed the cool, inviting cocktail. I quickly ordered two more. "Why did you order two?" he said, looking puzzled.

"When I drink I always have two drinks going as I don't want to sit and wait for one to be made."

That should have warned him about what was to come.

It was not long before I went into blackout. The next thing I remember was throwing up with my head in the ladies' toilet. The bastards must have taken me to the club in one of their unmarked police cars, but they decided to leave me there. I was so sick I couldn't stop dry retching. Staggering outside, I manoeuvred my way down the footpath. The Royal was locked for the night so I stayed at the nearest hotel. They must have been amused at how pissed I was.

The next morning, after going back to the pub to clean up, I dragged myself into the office. Bill was the only one there. He looked really crook too; it must have been a big session. "I'm here to answer the phone in case anyone rings," he said unenthusiastically. "You go back to the pub and sleep, or go up to the hospital and get a vitamin B injection. That's what I always do when I'm as crook as you look."

"No, thanks. I've never missed work because of the grog and I'm not going to start now."

It wasn't long before I regretted rejecting his offer to go home. "You *are* a real alcoholic," Bill stated a couple of hours later, in a tone that suggested he thought I had been pulling his leg earlier. He never asked me to have a drink again and I found out quick smart where the meetings of Alcoholics Anonymous were.

Back at home, Irene hit the roof when I eventually told her I was an alcoholic and that I was not going to drink again, a day at a time. There was lots of yelling and screaming with things thrown around for added effect. John just sat in his lounge chair rolling cigarettes and mumbling to himself. He didn't give a damn as long as *he* didn't have to stop drinking.

After Irene's last go at giving up the grog, the night before my tenth birthday when she had suffered a heart attack, the doctors had wanted to perform a liver biopsy on her. She had refused, knowing her liver was stuffed. The heart attack did scare her, however, and she remained sober for two years because of her fear of needing a liver biopsy. Of course if *she* couldn't drink, neither could John. Those were two very hard years. Living in a house with two dry drunks is much worse than active alcoholism. Fortunately old Shep the little brown and white corgi died, and in her grief Irene took up the grog again. John was very grateful because he could drink again too, and in no time they were splitting up flagons of McWilliams port as usual.

Now here I was, announcing I wasn't going to drink any more. Irene was convinced that Greg, this bloody suit-wearing new boyfriend, had been a bad influence. Irene had bullied me into getting rid of potential husbands in the past whenever she found them to be a real threat. But this time the jig was up. Months of meetings had given me knowledge, and *that* is power.

On a gut level I knew that Greg was the best thing to ever happen to me. If I threw away this chance at happiness, I would die. I was fighting for my life. I deserved to get married and have children, to have a crack at life. I couldn't stay and clean up after Irene and John any more, watching them die while they sucked the life out of me. And Irene was smart enough to know what Greg meant; she knew she was fighting for life too. It was vicious.

On 4 December 1990 I was sitting at my desk in the task force office. Bill called me over and said, "Debbie, I want you take out a search warrant." He handed me a piece of paper with some information and an address. This search warrant was directed at one of the main targets of the operation. "Type up the warrant now and apply for it straight away."

"Okay."

"You can execute the warrants with a couple of the boys this afternoon."

I typed up some search warrant applications with the information Bill had provided. Then it was down to the chamber magistrate at the local court to swear the warrants out. We raided the office early that afternoon. No one seemed surprised that the police were on the doorstep. The search didn't take as long as expected. One green folder containing a few papers was handed over. The rest of the office was devoid of records, which could be considered unusual for a companies registered office.

On 14 January 1991 I went down to the Wollongong police station with a colleague to take a statement from an employee of the company on which I'd executed the search warrant. He had information that the company had been tipped off about the search warrant the night before it was executed. They had time to take some of the relevant documents to a nearby hotel before the police got there.

A week later I went down to the hotel to speak to the manager and examined the register with no success. Nobody seemed to remember any guests carrying boxes of documents on that night. Maybe they just didn't feel like being helpful. In the end nothing was ever done about this allegation – yet how could the targets be tipped off the night before when the decision to do the raid hadn't been made until that day?

Things were very cosy for the boys living away from home. One one occasion I came in to find a thin white stain on the blue webbed material of my office chair. All the boys thought it was funny and told me to be careful not to get pregnant. Everybody played up. One guy told his wife she could only ring him at the office because the granny flat where he was staying did not have a phone. In actual fact he was shacked up with a sexy local goddess who was into bondage. Apparently she liked the slave and master games and referred to herself as his sex slave. In the office she was known as 'slave' for short.

Bernie on the other hand only played up when he'd had too much to drink. He kept running into one particular girl around the traps, as Wollongong is not a big place. She really had the hots for him. Apparently on one night of passion he ran into the surf with his good suit pants and shoes on. Her special name for him was 'Chocky Eyes' which was the running joke around the office.

One fateful night Bill organised a big dinner at a Chinese restaurant. Bernie, Paul and I were filling in time at the pub before it was time to go to the restaurant. I was drinking my boring Coke as usual. Paul had gone to the bar to order the next round.

"So, Bernie," I said with a smile, "what are your plans after dinner?"

"Nothing much."

"Going to catch up with the girl? Eh, Chocky Eyes?"

He leaned over and slapped my face. Hard. This took me totally by surprise. He then pointed at me and said, "Don't you ever call me that again," in a cold, menacing tone. My face stung and tears began to swell in my eyes.

Paul came back from the bar to find me with my head down, unable to talk. Bernie snapped back into his jovial self, as if he had just pulled his ugly head off in time for Paul's return. The side of my face was stinging from the blow. I was devastated and scared; Bernie was a large man and that blow had nearly knocked me down. Now I was very scared of him.

After that round those two left for the restaurant. "I'll catch up with you at the restaurant," I told them. "You go ahead."

Wandering back to the police car, I sat crying in stunned disbelief for about half an hour. I didn't know what to do.

At the restaurant I sat without saying anything. "Are you all right?" someone asked.

"I have a headache."

Before the second course I got up and went home.

I sat on the edge of the bed in my room weighing up the situation. The whole incident had shocked me, and I didn't want any more trouble. I knew I wouldn't tell anyone at work what had happened, partly because I didn't want to give Bernie the satisfaction of knowing that he had hurt me. I also felt I had so many problems already that the last thing I wanted to do was add to them. I now know that this reluctance to speak out is typical for abuse victims and people with post-traumatic stress. I would behave very differently now.

When Greg came to collect me to take me home for my holidays, I couldn't even tell him that Bernie had slapped my face. The next morning in a flood of tears I was able to get the words out.

Greg was furious. He was straight on the phone to Bill. "Do you know that Bernie assaulted Deb the other night?"

"Yeah, he told me about it."

"Well, what are you going to do about it?"

"There were other people there. Bernie said she provoked him."

"Calling someone 'Chocky Eyes' is not provocation."

"Well, Bernie's got people to back him up."

"If Bernie ever touches Debbie again he will be answering to me. Keep your boys under control, Bill, or there will be trouble. Do you understand me?"

I was very upset, but felt safer now that for the first time in my life I had someone who loved and protected me. I had been the adult and the rescuer all the time before now. This was a great new feeling.

In January of 1991, before returning to the Fraud Squad from Task Force Mort, I had undertaken an investigation for which I was the 'informant' and 'officer in charge of the matter'. It eventually came up for trial after my return to the Fraud Squad. I had one of the solicitors from the office of the Director for Public Prosecutions checking to see if the brief had been prepared. Having repeatedly been told that Bill and Bernie had completed it, I wasn't worried but I rang the 'Rort' office just to make sure.

There was silence at the other end of the phone. "Sorry, Deb, it hasn't been finished," came the voice of one of the young detectives who had replaced me.

"What do you mean? They told me it was completed."

"They deliberately left it sitting on your old desk so that it would not be prepared in time for the trial."

"This is bullshit."

"They did it deliberately as a payback for speaking out about Bernie slapping your face."

Something would have to be done quickly or I would be facing possible departmental charges for neglect of duty. I went in search of George McTaggart.

"George, I need to go down to Wollongong for a couple of days," I told him. "I've just found out that the brief I was working on has not been finished. I need to get it ready for court."

"They told me the brief was completed."

"That's what they told me, too. But they just left it on my desk and did nothing with it. I need to go up and finish it or I'll be in trouble with the DPP."

"Well, that's your problem. You should have made sure it was finished. You're not going to Wollongong just to fix it."

I thought George knew that Bill and Bernie were trying to make me look bad. I would have to do something to fix this mess myself. In the end I was sent to Wollongong on the day of the trial and frantically prepared the matter for court. I had telephoned a few people ahead of time and arranged for documents and other statements to be ready. The paperwork was collated and ready just in time

At about this time, a girlfriend won a trip to Fiji and asked me to go with her. I was about to pack when Irene pulled her usual trick of bringing undone anything nice for me. "The doctor wants us to go into hospital," she announced. "But I'm not going in unless you sit with us and wait until we are admitted." I couldn't believe it; here was a free trip to Fiji going down the drain. I wanted to say 'No' to her for the first time in my life, yet I had a gut feeling that I had to save them and get them into hospital.

The next morning I went to Mascot airport with Greg. In the airport lounge Jenny had a big smile on her face, but looked confused when she saw we weren't carrying any luggage. I explained as best I could: "Look, I have to put my folks into hospital. Irene is bright Henny Penny yellow and you know what John looks like. The walking dead."

Jenny was pretty good about it all, but I felt so guilty, not to mention ripped off. Letting Jenny down at the last minute was bad, she had won the trip for two and now the spare ticket was wasted.

Back at home I got Irene and John ready to go to hospital. We arrived at Hornsby hospital at about 10am and were kept waiting until about eight that evening. The young registrar finally examined them. "They're not that sick," he decided after a couple of minutes. "They don't need to be admitted."

"They're not that sick? Just look at them. My mother is canary yellow!"

"Bring them back in if they get worse."

"Listen, sunshine, I've been waiting here about ten hours to get them admitted. I'm not going anywhere until they have a bed."

He scurried off and spoke to one of the nursing sisters. She came over and said, "Follow me to Ward 12."

Finally, they were taken into different wards. What a long, embarrassing and depressing day that was. Alcoholics are rarely treated with respect by the medical fraternity. I have been talked to like scum by hospital staff ignorant of the disease. My parents, and any other alcoholics for that matter, are still human beings. When they were little kids they didn't ask to end up on the human scrapheap.

While John and Irene were in hospital I visited them every day, which was expected of me, though I resented it, considering their behaviour when I was in hospital with the ectopic pregnancy.

On the fifth day I saw Irene lying in bed, and reached over and touched her shoulder to wake her up. But I couldn't. She was in a coma. I ran for the nurse at the front counter and told her my mother was unconscious. Within seconds she was being rushed to intensive care.

They managed to bring her round about two days later and John was brought to the intensive care unit in a wheelchair to see her. Greg was there, as well as my brother and a few close friends. Irene was awake, chatting away, and apparently very sharp, unable to believe she had been in a coma at all. Not for the first time, she promised me she would never drink scotch again. She had learned her lesson this time and her drinking days were behind her. John was heartbroken. He had a big tube coming out of his lung to drain the fluid off into a big glass bottle. They were both in a dreadful state. Irene was only fifty-nine years old, John sixty-three. Yet they had the bodies of ninety-year-olds.

We said goodbye to Irene and were all standing outside the intensive care ward when the alarms went off. The sound meant that one of the patients had stopped breathing. I tiptoed back into the ward, praying that it wasn't my girl. Irene was lying there with people all around trying to save her. Running back out I told the others; we could do nothing but wait. Within ten minutes we were called back in. Irene had died. I couldn't believe it; we had been talking minutes before, and now she was dead. I wanted to die on the spot.

They brought John back in his wheelchair to be with her and we held hands over her yellow, bloated body. John's hands were just skin and bone. He just cried quietly. He and Irene had drunk and fought together for forty-three years, and now she was gone.

Four weeks later it was 12 April, my birthday, and I felt suicidal. The guys at the Fraud Squad were giving me a hard time, even though I had just buried my mother. I couldn't take any more and ran out of the office, deciding to go to Hornsby hospital, see John one more time and then kill myself. I was approaching his ward when his doctor came up and said, "We have just put your father on a pethidine drip. We know he is in a lot of pain, but he won't admit it. He is one of those old bushies who thinks you have to put up with it. He is not going to last very long."

This pulled me out of the suicide dive and back into reality. I sat by his bed holding his hand. He rolled his head towards me. "I just want to be with Ike," he said, which is what he always called Irene. Moments later, he too was dead.

We buried them together in the lawn cemetery at Rouse Hill with John's parents. I also bought two more graves, one for Greg and one for myself. Greg always jokes that I have to die first, as he does not want to spend the rest of eternity next to my mother.

John left me the old farmhouse in his will. I deserved it, as it would not have been there if it was not for my sweat. No one wanted to know about John and Irene when they were alive, but after they died all the family vultures came out of hiding. I choose not to have contact with my family these days.

During all my time at the Fraud Squad I hadn't been teamed up with a partner. In mid July 1991, after complaining to Jamison that I had been at the section for fourteen months without one, I was allocated Detective Senior Constable Kenneth Ridley for approximately eleven weeks, after which he was transferred out of the section. In December, after repeated requests, I was allocated Detective Senior Constable Graeme Cunynghame as a partner. This only lasted for eleven days as he was already on the way out of the unit. Both men said they were very happy to work with me, which cut across George McTaggart's comment: "How can we expect someone to work with you when you are sleeping with Greg Locke?"

Graeme Cunynghame said to me: "Write everything they are doing to you in your duty book, so it's all dated and you don't forget anything." It was a great piece of advice.

CHAPTER 15

ALL GOOD MATES

In late December 1991 I was contacted by a divisional detective attached to Windsor police station, a substation of Parramatta. "I have a brief on Jim Marowitz," he explained. "It's about the break and enter you did a while ago. I need to get a statement from you."

"Why do you want a statement after all this time?"

"It relates to a fraudulent car insurance claim."

Although this seemed like a minor issue, I believed I was finally to be interviewed about the information I had given. It hadn't dawned on me how weird it was to be speaking to a constable from Windsor, not somebody from Headquarters.

The leak that I was to give a statement was instantaneous. Ron Marowitz rang me at home on 23 December 1991, at around 8.45pm. I was surprised he had my number. While he was talking to me I made notes of what he said because I was so scared of him, particularly because of the criminal contacts he had.

"The boss of Parramatta Detectives rang me. He wants my duty books for 1988. Do you know what it's about?"

"I have no idea," I lied.

"I think I know what it's about now. Something I did with my brother but I didn't think you were there. My brother's girlfriend put us into the ombudsman. Did you do a break 'n' enter at her flat? I'm not sure if you were there."

"Should we be talking about this?"

"You're right, I'll ring you back."

Ten minutes later he called back. "Yeah, I think my phone's bugged," he said. "Look for your book tomorrow. I'm going to go and get mine. I've been off for seven months and they're still trying to get me. I'm working for private enterprise now, it's not easy. I'll meet you outside the Remington building and we can get our heads together. We want to get our stories straight before IPSU talk to us. Are you sure you never met my brother?"

"Maybe, I can't remember. I'll speak to you later."

As soon as he hung up I got the pager number for Superintendent Bob Myers from the Duty Operations inspector, and told him about my conversation with Ron. Myers told me not to meet Ron the following day

I rang Myers again the next day. "I think I know how Ron has found out about the interview," he told me. "I had asked an ex-IPSU officer at Parramatta to obtain the information needed confidentially. He should have known better than to speak to the boss. I will have strong words with the boss for tipping Ron off."

Myers then gave me a phone number to ring, so that the Police Department would foot the bill for getting me a silent number. I never heard from Ron again, which makes me think he was told that I reported our phone call immediately.

On 2 January 1992 I went to Windsor police station, driving all the way out on my own, to make my statement of complaint. It was a traumatic experience. The office was overloaded and I was in full view and hearing of everyone in the room. I was being interviewed as a whistleblower, which might have explained the dark figure who was standing in the corner, watching the proceedings. Detective Chief Inspector Wladimir Golowenko stood there, as did Inspector Stuart McFadden and another senior officer. McFadden and this man had come out to Glenorie when Irene and Uncle Bill put on the BBQ spectacle, a memory that still makes me cringe.

A few weeks after my statement at Windsor was taken I ran into Constable First Class Lisa Everett, a colleague from Parramatta days. "I was at a send-off the other day," she said. "Ron was telling everyone you'd made a statement, and what was in it." I immediately telephoned Windsor police station, asking where the leak had come from. Laughter greeted me from the other end of the phone. "Yes, well, it's one of two people and I think I know which one it was."

I was just dumbfounded. Every time I reported to internal investigators, Ron was told what I said. Soon I started receiving really abusive phone calls. Some featured a woman's voice giggling with noises in the background, as if the call was being made from a bar.

One day Ron walked into the office. I nearly fainted. I had no idea what to expect next. By this point I had told Greg all the details of what had happened at Parramatta. On separate occasions both Greg and I discussed with the head of the Fraud Squad, our concern at having Marowitz working there. Greg also told me that he discussed with Jamison the fact that Ron knew all about my allegations against him, and the anxiety his transfer to the section would cause me.

A short time later Ron was attached to the Solicitors Unit of the Fraud Squad. When I saw him seated in his shirt and tie with the rest of his team, I thought I was going to die. He appeared so relaxed, as if he had been with the squad for years. But only a matter of days later he was suspended from duty over his actions in relation to a shooting incident in an illegal casino. Having dismissed what we said, the boss now had the embarrassment of seeing one of his officers suspended over corruption allegations.

Greg and I were now living in a beautiful old Victorian house in Birchgrove, and would catch the ferry to work together. It was the best time of our romance. Then I became pregnant.

Greg's mother Margaret said, "You don't have to rush to get married."

I said, "Yes, I am giving this baby a name."

"Will you keep your maiden name? All the young girls do these days."

I looked at her in shock. A great way to say, 'Welcome to the family.'

In an effort to make things easier at the section we invited George McTaggart to be MC at our wedding. He declined. I tried so hard to get on the good side of old George, but it was to no avail.

I was so down and flat that I even told Greg I just wanted to get married in a registry office, with no fuss or drama. Greg was horrified. He pointed out that I would be just repeating history, with shame of the kind Irene had experienced in her black dress. He put his foot down and demanded that we go the whole hog. So with the help of the Yellow Pages, I organised the wedding in one afternoon. I did it from a hospital bed, an amazing feat; I was green all through my pregnancy and couldn't stop throwing up. The placenta was breaking away, causing bleeding and several spells in hospital.

Greg and I were married on 15 February 1992 at St Jude's church, Randwick. The wedding was one of the highlights of my life. I wore the most beautiful satin dress with a long veil. Michael Drury asked a friend of his who was a police chaplain, the Reverend Peter Mumford, to perform the ceremony. It was a beautiful service, made more special by having as bridesmaids Claudia Campanelli and Mary, another old friend with whom I had gone through the Police Academy.

It rained solidly for the two weeks before 15 February. I thought to myself that this was not a good omen. But while I was at the hairdresser's that morning with my bridesmaids, someone came into the salon and said, "The rain's stopped." I couldn't believe it. We were so lucky. I had my mother's brother walk me down the aisle. It was good of him, yet it was not the same as having my father do it. I couldn't believe Irene and John were not there for my big day, even though I knew there mightn't have been a wedding if they had been alive. I had a photo of them on the table near the wedding cake.

We had the reception with 120 guests in the Members' Pavilion at the Sydney Cricket Ground. Few were family. Michael Drury was kind enough to be MC for the night for us. A friend from Greg's days in the Police Pipe Band piped us into the church and reception. We had a large white Cadillac limousine and all the trappings.

I was so grateful that for the first time in my life someone loved and cared for me. "You have to be a princess for a day," Greg said. It was fantastic. Yet I did feel green the whole night. I said to Greg, "When we are married for ten years, we are going to do this all over again so I can eat and enjoy it." And we did.

The poor baby spent the whole wedding squashed up in a laced-up corset. When I got home that night and Greg, after much difficulty, got me out of the corset, my stomach was flat, even though I was five months pregnant. I was hysterical, sure I had killed the baby. But it must have turned during the night and next morning I looked huge, as if I was ten months pregnant. If the guests at the wedding had seen me at breakfast they would not have believed their eyes.

The doctor insisted that we cancel our honeymoon in Hawaii for medical reasons. Another disappointment, yet the wellbeing of my unborn baby was paramount. Instead, Greg took me to Bowral for the weekend and then to Canberra for a few days. I spent the whole time throwing up. It was the sickest part of my pregnancy. I felt ill, but I was very much in love, and I had a new name and a new life. I was now Deborah Locke. How strange it felt. It was a chance at a new beginning.

In my heart I knew I never would have had a chance at happiness if Irene and John had still been alive. Within a year of their dying I did the three things Irene, when sober, always said she wanted to see before she died: to see me married, have a daughter and finish university. It made me cry often. I now know this is a symptom of post-traumatic stress.

I was straight back to work at the Fraud Squad, yet things only got worse. Rome Martin, the senior sergeant, appeared to be highly resentful of the fact that women were allowed maternity leave. He would say, "Maternity leave is just prostitution. You're being paid to lie on your back." It was a comment quoted in the *Sydney Morning Herald* some time later under very different circumstances, and it has come to haunt him.

The old boys really turned it on. Their opinion was that my career was definitely over now, so they were letting me have it with both barrels. In *their* day when a woman became engaged she had to leave the job. These guys just didn't understand that they were dinosaurs, that the world had moved on while they were in their time warp at the Fraud Squad. It wasn't for nothing that the Fraud Squad was sometimes called Jurassic Park.

Sick throughout my pregnancy, I had to be hospitalised on a number of occasions. I know I was never expected to come back, nor was I wanted. But I wasn't entirely without friends at work. During this time I went up to the office of a fat old detective who did paperwork for the Task Force Group on the floor above. He was on desk duties and in his spare time was studying to become a psychologist. He had heard of the harassment I was undergoing and told me that he had made notes in his diary about it.

In April 1992 Jamison and McTaggart made me prepare a written report concerning one of the briefs I was working on.

Written update reports were not usually required. Luckily I had kept very careful notes and could easily do it, so they couldn't get me out on the grounds that I wasn't working. When I tried to give a copy of my report to Rome Martin he said, "I'm not part of this," and would not accept a copy. I think he realised the harassment had gone too far.

Being pregnant with Vanessa should have been the happiest time of my life; instead it was a bloody nightmare. Once I put my head down on the table as I was feeling so ill, and had to cop a barrage of abuse. On another occasion when I was being yelled at and I started bleeding, Claudia rushed me to the Mater hospital at Crows Nest. An ultrasound showed that part of the placenta was breaking away. I had a few days' bed rest in hospital while everything settled down.

I took maternity leave in mid July 1992 and Vanessa was born two weeks later on 1 August. I worked right up to the due birth date, as I wanted to show how dedicated I was to my job, not that it did me any good. Vanessa was an emergency caesarean; the pressure I was under for falling pregnant had taken its toll. We were very blessed that she was okay.

Vanessa added perfect joy to our lives, yet I was soon to find myself in a new battleground. It had been less than twelve months since I lost both my parents, yet I had no support from Greg's family or from mine.

After I came out of hospital, Greg's mother came to stay, supposedly to help with the baby. On the first night after I helped make dinner, she said, "Go to sleep and I will bring Vanessa in to her cot later." I was exhausted and quickly fell asleep. In the morning I awoke to find the cot empty. I was hysterical. I ran out into the lounge room and found a note: "Don't worry about Vanessa, I put her in bed with me for the night. I have fed her formula."

I couldn't believe it. I ran into the other bedroom and here they were in bed asleep. I grabbed my daughter in a panic and took her into the bedroom to feed from my painful engorged breasts. Tears ran down my face. It was such an act of betrayal, and I knew it was because of my history. Nobody in Greg's family has ever seen me take a drink, yet they still considered me an unfit mother.

It beats me what people think an alcoholic is. Most think they are deros in dirty overcoats. But some of those I know are the most powerful and wealthy people in our society. You would never pick them because they are sober, in recovery. They are the same as everybody else, the only thing they can't do is drink.

It was bad enough that I was grieving the loss of my parents, but to try and take my child was, and is, unforgivable. I am a good mother. My children only know me as sober. I love them. They are the light of my life. I only drank before to dull the pain. Now I have new coping skills, such as prayer and meditation.

While on maternity leave I decided to telephone Jamison. "I want to come back to work soon," I told him, "but I need you to do something about the way I'm being treated."

"I'll speak to the blokes, but there's not much I can do about their attitude," he said. "They have just been here too long."

"Okay Debbie, I'll tell you what I'll do," he added. "If you come back early from maternity leave I will put you together with Sue Newcombe. She is coming back from maternity leave on the eighth of February. Things will be better."

Taking Jamison's assurances seriously, I returned to work from maternity leave after six months instead of the approved twelve. I felt that if I demonstrated I was keen they would be impressed and my work environment would improve. I wanted to show them that I took my job seriously and that having a child was not the end of my career.

A week before I went back, however, I discovered I was pregnant again.

Then, immediately upon my return to the section, I was marched into the kitchen by two of the officers. They stood over me after indicating that I should sit down. "You're a burden, you should not have come back," they told me. "You won't be travelling ever again. You won't be working with Sue, but you can assist Charlie and his partner Frank."

I began sobbing in the chair while they stood over me. People in the general office could hear what was going on, yet no one ever supported me over what happened that day. They were all too scared; most of them had wives and mortgages. I was told that, even though I would be working with Charlie and Frank, I wasn't allowed to sit with them. Instead I was to sit near George at the front of the room, where he could supervise me.

I didn't even have a real desk; it was more like part of a workstation. I was not allowed to have a telephone, the reason being, "She just nags on the bloody phone all the time." It was also almost impossible to get a police vehicle so I could leave the office to interview witnesses. Every time I answered a telephone,

George demanded to know the nature of the call. A lot of derogatory comments were made in relation to my second pregnancy and the amount of work I was doing.

I continued to document all these incidents of harassment in my official police diary. I did not care if anyone in the office read my words, as everything was true. Every couple of weeks George or Rome would tick each entry and sign the diary as being correct without ever bothering to read what I had written. I held my breath every time they checked the diary, waiting for everything to blow up, but amazingly it never did. If they had bothered to do their job properly I would have been in trouble; my diary was an official police document.

In March 1993, because of the stress I was under, I withdrew from a Bachelor of Social Science (Psychology) degree I had been attempting to do on a part-time basis. Then in late March 1993 I had a miscarriage and went off on sick report. I cried and cried, and said to Greg, "Those bastards will pay for what they have done."

My kind doctor in Mosman conducted several tests upon the baby girl, looking for underlying causes of the miscarriage, but none was found. He wrote a report speculating that emotional and physical stress in the early weeks of pregnancy could have been a significant contributing factor. I had on previous occasions complained to him about how my bosses were treating me.

I still grieve the loss of my daughter. Vanessa should have grown up with the sister she lost.

I came out of hospital only two days before Vanessa's christening. All the invitations had been sent out, I was not going to go through any more embarrassment, so it was on with the show. Greg was against it, thinking I wasn't up to it, but I was adamant. I had an Indian lady looking after the house and Vanessa at the time so we decided to have an Indian banquet. Greg and I love trying aspects of different cultures.

I was feeling very shaky from the anaesthetic and it had only been ten months since I last had a drink. I kept having little slips every time I had a crisis and was still considered very new in recovery. I was finally tipped over the edge when Greg's parents came late and then went into the back lane to consume sandwiches they had brought, saying, "We don't eat black people's food." Greg's grandmother rang later that evening to tell me of her disapproval of the whole affair, what with the drunken behaviour of the black people, etc. My guests did not even drink, so she was way off the mark. I lost it and told her off. It was all too much for me and I stormed out.

Walking up the road in a state I saw my next-door neighbour Duncan sitting in the local Thai restaurant. I walked in and sat down.

I said, "Order me a double."

He said, "But you don't drink."

"I do now." I then proceeded to try and have a drink with Duncan in every pub in Balmain. This was beyond even my ability, but we had fun of a kind trying.

I don't know what time it was when I arrived back home. I jumped into bed and started giggling. Greg said, "What are you laughing for?"

"I made it back." I should have gone to sleep, but I must have gone into blackout. The next thing I remember is sitting on the lounge room floor in the dark, trying to open a commemorative bottle of port with a large carving knife. When Greg took it from me I started hitting my head against the floor. He kicked a cushion under my head, which made me laugh.

The only way Greg could get me back to bed was to let me break the thing I loved most in the world. It was a statue of three Muses. It was stamped on the bottom and was the family heirloom. Irene had bought it off a druggie down the Cross when I was a kid. It was to be passed down the family. Greg negotiated that the front window be opened before I threw it out. Then I was satisfied. I had hurt myself sufficiently to go back to bed.

The next morning I could hardly get my head off the pillow. It was the first time Greg had really been angry about my drinking. I promised him I was never going to drink again, and he just looked at me with contempt. He had heard that one before. What he didn't know then was that I really meant it. I had had my last drink.

The neighbours couldn't understand why there was a smashed statue out on the front footpath. I tried to tell them I was an alcoholic, and they just wouldn't believe me. They even argued with me about it over eggs and bacon at a restaurant. Some people just can't believe that some women should not drink. Thank God I have not had a drink since that day. I am very aware now that I am more vulnerable after an anaesthetic or a major upset. I always get myself straight to a meeting when things are a bit tough. One day at a time.

CHAPTER 16

IT HITS THE FAN

Before Terry Jamison, one of the heads of the Fraud Squad had been a famous old boy named Nelson Chad, who had been sacked for misconduct. Nelson took dismissal in his stride, went out and started a private inquiry agency in his daughter's name. He needed the resources of the Fraud Squad to run his business, so he had a lot of contact with them. The investigation company, Satinvale, ran some private investigations for a major insurance company, and I thought McTaggart and Jamison gave priority to these briefs. Not everybody agreed with them; I heard plenty of complaints from my colleagues about having to do work for Chad.

In the normal course of events Jamison would receive a brief and add it to the whiteboard next to his desk. There would be twenty to thirty jobs under investigation at any one time. He had them all on Dymo labels on little magnetic strips, stuck on the board. The jobs then just sat there, waiting to be allocated to someone. As far as I could see, once they were allocated they would then be entered into the Fraud Squad job book. Chad's work wouldn't necessarily go onto the whiteboard or subsequently into the job book at all. Those jobs would only appear in their duty books if they had to travel.

Early in June 1993 I was having a conversation in the foyer of the Sydney Police Centre with a victim of crime when Sergeant Kim Cook came up. "I've got to talk to you now," he said. It had been two years since I confided my problems to him, telling him how I was being treated, the story of my time at Wollongong and details of the mismanagement and corruption I suspected were happening in the Fraud Squad. So when Cook approached me he already knew some of my complaints.

He had endured a rough time since last I saw him. He had been assaulted a few times and his house had been broken into. There was a campaign against him, which was making his life a misery – more so because he had to think of his wife and two little girls. His story was now in the hands of ICAC (the Independent Commission Against Corruption). Now he needed someone to corroborate his statements that the police culture was really as bad as he was claiming.

I didn't know all this at the time. We talked for a while in the foyer. Soon John Deerfield joined us at the takeaway bistro inside the front door. Deerfield didn't get involved in our conversation; he just sat there, drinking his coffee, while Kim and I talked. Because I had given Kim a certain amount of detail in March 1991, I felt that our talk this time was no more than a catch-up session.

I told him about my miscarriage and my six-month-old daughter; I was only a couple of months sober again after my one-night bust, and with all the hormone changes and the way I was being treated I was in a very vulnerable state. I told him how very stressed I was, about my treatment as a whistleblower and my harassment as a female officer. It was nice to talk to someone who appeared to care about my wellbeing, and over our cappuccinos I had a good old whinge.

Kim asked me again about Wollongong, and whether things had changed much since his own stint there. He asked me to go into a lot of detail about McTaggart and Nelson Chad and about Jamison and the way the Fraud Squad was being run.

Without my knowledge, on 10 June 1993 Kim reported our conversation to Chief Inspector Dan Dillon, staff officer at Professional Responsibility. This was the part of the service that had the Professional Integrity Branch (PIB, formerly known as the Internal Police Security Unit) and Internal Affairs as different areas under its overall command. The PIB was meant to investigate more serious corruption matters than the general internal complaints handled by Internal Affairs.

When I found out what Kim had done, I was panic-stricken. After my experience at Parramatta I had no wish to lodge a complaint with the Professional Integrity Branch. I didn't want to report on the Fraud Squad while I was still working there and I didn't want to leave, despite the problems I was having. I liked working regular office hours, and I did not want the boys to force me out. Despite my grave misgivings at the time I am now glad that it all came out in the open.

When it was leaked straight back to the Fraud Squad that there had been a complaint due to my information, I was numb with shock. Greg kept trying to calm me down, "It doesn't matter, Kim Cook is the one who's gone to Dillon at PIB, not you."

"But he's not the one who's passed on the information!" I was distraught. "If I hadn't told Cook all that was going on, he wouldn't have had anything to go and report. They'll be so angry with me!"

I was right, they were very bloody angry. No one mentioned Kim Cook's name again. It was all down to bloody stupid Debbie, they thought. How could she do this to us? What was she thinking?

After my conversation with Kim in the bistro I received a telephone call from Sergeant Peter Nunan of PIB. "I want to speak to you about your complaints concerning the Fraud Squad. Can I interview you at home on June twenty-first?"

"Do I have to? I don't want to make any complaints. That was Kim's idea."

"I have a directive memorandum, so you have no choice." My heart sank. I had never intended to lodge a formal complaint, but now it seemed I had to submit to a written interview, which effectively meant making a complaint in writing.

I did the written interview at my home in Balmain, typing the answers to questions on a laptop. It took a long time. I remember looking at Vanessa asleep on the brown leather lounge, wrapped in her pink bunny blanket. She was so beautiful, innocent and safe for the time being from all this rubbish. When I had finished Nunan discovered that he couldn't print the document, so we went back to the PIB office at North Sydney. While we were at the PIB he asked me a number of further questions. He then printed up those questions and my answers and gave me a copy.

I told Nunan about false travel allowance claims by Jamison; mismanagement of Task Force Mort in Wollongong; McTaggart directing junior officers to access the computer system to obtain vehicle registrations; information being supplied to and work being referred to Chad; Bill Gould's inappropriate allocation of travel allowance; and sexual harassment and equal opportunity issues.

By 22 June, the day after I was interviewed, the people at the Fraud Squad knew that I had gone to PIB. Jamison kept glaring at me and McTaggart took his first day off sick in twelve years with a stress-related headache. At one stage a colleague responded to a comment of mine with, "Why don't you go and report that to Professional Integrity?"

On 28 June at eight in the morning, Jamison gave a talk about what officers should do if they felt there was corruption in the Fraud Squad or if they had any EEO problems. He produced a booklet called 'Fraud Squad Anti-Corruption Plan'. This was the first time we had ever had a meeting of this sort. The booklet and the talk covered all the issues I had mentioned in my PIB interview.

But I wasn't there; that day I had been told not to come into work until ten. A copy of the booklet was placed in every pigeonhole but mine. Greg and his partner Detective Senior Constable Bruce Van Der Graaf were the only other members of the section who were not told about the meeting. They had been sent downtown to work out of the St James building on the Police GIO Task Force.

Later that day I was to be summoned to ICAC to be interviewed. As I was putting things in my handbag ready to leave, Charlie, one of my colleagues, strolled up and said, "Have you got your gun with you?"

"Why?"

"You better take it with you or someone here might use it on you."

He looked over to McTaggart who had Jamison standing just behind him. Was this a warning? Intimidation?

At ICAC John Warburton asked me first about Cook, and then about the Fraud Squad. Seeing my hesitation, he said, "You don't have to answer my questions." I said that, having already been interviewed by PIB, I didn't want to say any more about the Fraud Squad. Because ICAC had no power to direct me to answer questions, I didn't talk to them about the Fraud Squad at all. I was still very upset because of Charlie's death threat.

Early the next morning, 29 June, I rang Sergeant Nunan at PIB about the leak. I also told him about the death threat. "I'll make a report of it," he said. "When can you come in?"

We arranged to meet in North Sydney at lunchtime that day. As I walked out of the police building on my way to the station, I saw Jamison watching me, a very black look on his face. My hands sweated but I put my head up and kept walking.

While I spoke to Nunan, I noticed that he didn't ask me to put anything in writing, including my complaint about the leak back to the Fraud Squad and the death threat; I didn't know whether my words were to be treated as a formal complaint. While I was with Nunan, Dan Dillon came in, looking very upset. He and McTaggart were friends and he acted as if he thought I'd accused him of the leak. "The brief is over at Headquarters now," he said. "I'll make sure your name doesn't go on it so the Fraud Squad can't see that you're the informant."

"But they already know," I said.

When I left PIB I went up the road to a public telephone box and telephoned Inspector John Graham, head of the Welfare Unit. He was a nice kind bloke who had been a big bear in his day, but now he was tired, waiting out his time like many others. He had lived near Glenorie when I was a kid, and I'd known him for years. He had also been in the Police Pipe Band with Greg. I told him everything that was going on and made arrangements to see him the next day.

When I did, I gave him one of Jamison's booklets. He later told me that Jamison had approached him to give evidence against me, but Graham had refused to hear him out. It was the best support he could give me; he just wasn't interested in getting involved in the mess.

I was at home about two in the afternoon of 30 June when Nunan called. "Myatt, the boss, wants to talk to you right now. Can you get here by half past two?"

It was a big rush to get to North Sydney by 2.30 but I made it. I went into the interview room with Nunan who said, "I've done the report." I took him to mean he had reported my complaints about the leak and the death threat. On his desk he placed an unsigned piece of A4 paper with typing on it.

Though he wouldn't let me read it, I saw my name so I knew it was about our conversation of the previous day.

Nunan escorted me into the boss's office. Robert Myatt met me at the door and dismissed Nunan, who had been about to give him the report. "You can rip it up," Myatt said, and Nunan's face fell. Considering that Myatt hadn't even heard my story, this seemed a rather casual attitude. Myatt must have worked out what I was thinking because he explained, "We don't want anything yet on paper, because it will have to go to the ombudsman. If you've got anything to say, ring me up."

I was a bit disconcerted. "Can you give me your phone number?"

"You can find it in the internal directory."

It was difficult to avoid the impression that Myatt was not particularly concerned about anything I might have to say. At one point he took a phone call and had a very long conversation with his son, keeping me sitting there. But according to detailed notes I took as soon as I got home, he did tell me they had 'done the wrong thing' by me in relation to Parramatta, that I should sit it out and if it got too bad I would be moved. My original complaints about the Fraud Squad would be referred to Internal Affairs, who would handle the matter. As for the leak, Myatt's opinion was that Kim Cook was to blame. "Kim's caused problems for a lot of people," he said.

The piece of paper that Nunan produced has never been found. As far as I am aware, Internal Affairs never investigated my complaints.

When I walked into the Fraud Squad after my meeting with Myatt, McTaggart commented across the room, "IA. That's only departmental . . . and you can talk your way out of that." He didn't have to spell it out any more clearly: the story of Myatt's referring my information down to the lesser unit of Internal Affairs had got back to the Fraud Squad even before I had.

If possible, the environment grew even worse. I was scared for my life; after all I had spent two years in hiding with another cop who had been shot. I was really going to get it this time. Sitting on the lounge, rocking Vanessa gently in my arms one evening, I began to sob. These were seasoned, hard-nosed detectives and I had attacked their honey pot. How were they going to make me pay? Could I protect my family?

I lodged a formal complaint with the ombudsman about Myatt and Nunan on 27 April 1994. They held an enquiry and released a preliminary report on its outcome on 27 February 1995.

Nearly three weeks after my interview with Myatt, on Monday 19 July 1993, Detective Senior Sergeant Eric Campbell from Internal Affairs rang me at work. Normally if I received a call like that I would call back from a public phone, being too nervous to talk on the phone in the office. But I wasn't given a chance to do that on this occasion. Campbell said, "Go in and tell Jamison right now that I'm going to interview you."

As I was going to be out of the office the following day, I told him he couldn't see me until Wednesday 21st. "Oh well, I'll interview you then. Now, go and tell Jamison."

"It's supposed to be a secret," I said; there was no way I wanted to tell Jamison I was being interviewed by Internal Affairs. My hands were clammy and my head was spinning.

"I'm going to give you five minutes because I'm going out shortly," he said. "I have to ring Jamison about something else, so you have to do it now or I'll tell him."

As I got up from the chair I nearly fell over, my legs were so weak. I pushed myself across the room towards Jamison's glass-partitioned office and stood in front of his big wooden desk like a naughty schoolgirl. "I have to go to Internal Affairs on Wednesday," I said.

"I already know about this matter," he replied. "Why have you done this? I just can't believe this from you."

I burst into tears right there in his office and stood there sobbing, my whole body shaking. Three walls of his office were constructed of glass, so it was called 'the fish bowl'. Everyone in the office could see me crying. Jamison took me out the front of the Sydney Police Centre, providing a spectacle for any police who had managed to miss my distressed state inside. I felt that he was really trying to make me pay.

My last day performing *real* police work was spent in the country with Dave Walton. We went on a long drive to get a statement. It was as if I knew it was the end. It was the longest day, I was so heartbroken. Dave had been a groomsman at our wedding. Greg and I had also supported him through the death of his father and a relationship breakdown. But when trouble came for us, he went to ground, as other people did.

I only received one telephone call of support. That was from Detective Sergeant Peter Fenwick late one night. He said, "I've heard what's happened at the Fraud Squad and what they are saying about you. I want you to know that if Joan and I can be of any support for you, a shoulder, we are there." It meant a lot to me, and still does. No one else came forward.

The interview with Campbell took place on Wednesday 21 July 1993. Senior Constable Michael Kenny from IA was the typist. Campbell did not ask me about my complaint of a leak from PIB or the death threat I had reported to Nunan on 29 June; I assumed these would be subjects of a separate investigation.

Campbell would ask a question and I would give him an answer. He then reworded my answer for Kenny to type, so very few of my actual words were recorded. I was particularly upset about the answers he put down as my response to Question 32. He had picked up my comment that it appeared certain members of staff seemed to be favoured in the allocation of jobs, and asked me to explain it. Who, he asked, were these 'certain members'? According to his record of interview, I said:

It just seems that the people who have been there the longest and have not got home commitments get the better quality jobs. I have no evidence to substantiate that there is any problem involving the allocation of jobs. There is no one specific person I wish to nominate . . . Both Sergeants *[whom I named in my conversation with Kim Cook]* have been at the Fraud Squad for quite some time and have the expertise and the ability to investigate large, involved inquiries. I expect the Commander has every right to allocate the jobs to whomever he wishes and there are Sergeants there that prefer not to travel because of family commitments.

This, and many of the other answers in the interview, are not phrased according to the way I speak. (I would never call Jamison 'the Commander' for a start.) Campbell was apparently in the army before he joined the police. You can hear his voice in the answers. I wanted to name names, but he wouldn't let me. By the time of this interview I did want to make a formal complaint about everything that was happening at the Fraud Squad. Not just my harassment matters, but the abuse of travelling allowance, the matters concerning Nelson Chad, and the mismanagement of the unit. They had all been brought up by Cook anyway, so I couldn't deny them. Now I wanted to get my version on paper.

At the end of the so-called interview, Campbell asked me to sign his record. I stalled, and we finally agreed – reluctantly on his part – that I would sign the following Monday when I was back at work.

Prior to the interview I had just been frightened but afterwards I felt really intimidated and angry. Over the next couple of days I spoke with several people, including Greg, about the way the interview had been conducted. The point to emphasise here is that the old 'he said, she said' was out the window with an officer typing the conversation. By this time in the history of the New South Wales Police, and after years of verballing suspects, officers were apparently not considered credible witnesses. Many an innocent person had gone to gaol on the say-so of an alleged confession given to a detective in a record of interview. As a result, all interviews of suspects of serious crimes were given using electronic equipment, such as audio and video tapes. This was to ensure the integrity of the interview.

But the cops still had one place where they were still typing their records of interview, and that was when they interviewed their own. Of course, the idea was to help keep their own out of trouble by helping with the answers. They couldn't verbal the general public any more, but *I* sure got it that day. I just couldn't believe I didn't have the same rights as a suspect.

Later on the phone to Harry Neyenhuys, a fellow cop and a friend, I said, "I don't know what I should do. Campbell's going to want me to sign the interview, but how can I? It's all bullshit."

He suggested I should ask a woman whom he knew from the Police Association to sit in for the rest of the interview. I took Harry's advice even though I had never heard of her. I asked another friend, Bruce Van Der Graaf, to attend as a witness.

On the morning of Monday 26 July I met this woman at the Police Association office in Elizabeth Street and we walked to Police Headquarters together. She seemed as hard as nails and I felt safer and more confident as I walked towards the Internal Affairs office.

Campbell was much better behaved with her present, and recorded my EEO complaints. After the interview was over, she advised me to sign the whole record, even though the first pages of the first day were not in my words. I did so, though I wasn't happy about it. I feel now that she did not give me good advice.

Early the following morning, I headed out the front door on my way to work. As I approached the bus stop, a navy blue

Commodore slowly rounded the corner of the side street. It pulled into the kerb beside me and the passenger door opened. "Get in the car," said the driver. It was Jamison. He looked very angry.

I looked into the sleepy faces of the people waiting for the bus, trying to make eye contact with someone, hoping somebody might later remember me getting into a dark blue car in case I was never seen again. I stepped into the vehicle. He was my boss after all, what could I do? Run?

As Jamison drove very fast towards the city I stared straight ahead, clutching my black leather handbag in my sweaty hands. "Why has this happened?" he shouted, leaning towards me. "Why didn't you come to me?"

"But I did come to you," I said. "I came to you lots of times."

He quietened down and said, "It's just the way of the job. You don't think you had a miscarriage because of the way you were treated?"

Not knowing what to say I noticed he had entered the traffic lanes to head towards the Fraud Squad office.

"No, you need to drop me off at Police Headquarters." Campbell had refused to give me a copy of my statement, and I had told him I would come and pick it up.

"What!" He couldn't believe it. "Not *three* days at Internal Affairs? What could you be saying?"

As he changed lanes again and headed towards Hyde Park, I instantly felt better. I knew I was going to get out of the car alive. By the time I got to the Internal Affairs office I was trembling.

When I asked to see Campbell, I was told that he was busy and that he was not coming out to speak to me. "Tell him I am not leaving until I get a copy of my record of interview," I said.

I waited for a while and eventually Mick Kenny, the typist for the first interview, came out. "He doesn't want to talk to you," he said. "Here is the copy you want."

I took the pieces of paper, feeling as if my legs were about to give under me. Talking a closer look at me, Kenny said, "What's wrong with you? Your face is all red and you have hives all over your neck. You don't look very well."

Becoming more and more angry about the way Jamison and now Campbell had just treated me, I went downstairs to the EEO office. They took one look at the state I was in and went and got me a chair and a glass of water. I felt as if I was at the end of the line. But everything was out in the open now, the Fraud Squad knew what I was saying about them. So, angry as I was, I decided to run with the lot.

I told Sergeant Beverley Alland what had happened. When I had finished Alland rang Jamison in front of me and said that I had attended her office in a very distressed state and that she had sent me home to rest for the day. When she replaced the receiver she said, "That will give him something to think about, sitting off your house."

Every morning from then on I became physically sick when I had to catch the morning bus, for fear that Jamison would be waiting for me again.

On Sunday 1 August I went to the Fraud Squad office in the middle of the night with Claudia Campanelli, intent on removing my stuff. I knew I had to get out, but I was too frightened and embarrassed to pack up my belongings during working hours. We packed up all my belongings and took photocopies of the briefs I had been working on. The following day I returned to Headquarters and told the EEO unit, "I've left the Fraud Squad. I just can't take the harassment there any longer."

That same day Dennis Percy, Beverley Alland, Chief Superintendent Geoffrey Hoggett from Internal Affairs and I had a meeting in Percy's office. I told Superintendent Hoggett that I wasn't happy about the way Campbell had conducted my interview. He suggested that Campbell should be taken off the case. I thought this was a good idea. Senior Sergeant Peter Fitzpatrick was put in charge.

After the meeting, Percy made enquiries about placing me elsewhere. Eventually he found a job for me at the Establishment Control Branch. I didn't know what this was like and was concerned that, after all my hard work at university, my career might go down the drain just because I had spoken out. "Don't worry," he said. "This won't hurt your career. You'll get good experience at different places."

On 3 August I made notes, setting out all the errors and omissions in Campbell's record of interview. I also made a list of people who could verify what I had said and a list of EEO issues. The following day Fitzpatrick conducted a record of interview with me on ERISP equipment (Electronically Recorded Interview Suspect Persons). The video did not work so there was just an audiotape. I sensed that Fitzpatrick didn't trust me. However, I was able to get him to record a lot of the problems with the Fraud Squad that hadn't been covered with

Campbell. I refused to let them type the interview because I wanted my words to be properly recorded.

When Senior Constable Marea Rayment heard what had been going on, she told me she had had a similar experience of harassment in the Fraud Squad five years earlier, during pregnancy. They had often said to her she should be barefoot and in the kitchen, she said, and like me she had been denied proper work to do. She was still angry at the job they had done on her because she was a woman.

Internal Affairs' investigation into the Fraud Squad was codenamed Operation Zebra. I understand the investigation into my complaints about the Fraud Squad was completed on 18 April 1994. IA's report on their findings was sent to the ombudsman's office. I know the ombudsman told IA they were not satisfied and asked for further investigations.

CHAPTER 17

BEING A
WHISTLEBLOWER

I started at the Establishment Control Branch on 2 August, the day after Vanessa's first birthday. If I had been hoping for proper work to do, I was mistaken; though a detective senior constable with many years' experience, all they would give me to do was photocopying and other menial tasks. Requests for a further transfer were refused. It was then I realised that if I wanted to get out of Establishment Control Branch and improve my working conditions, I would have to apply for positions myself.

I felt as if I was being punished yet again. From time to time officers from the Fraud Squad would come up to my work area and snigger while they pretended to get application forms for internal positions. On these occasions I wanted the earth to open up and swallow me.

With my career path basically going nowhere I approached Superintendent Reg White. He suggested I talk to Chief

Inspector Lola Scott. Chief Inspector Scott, who was a single woman, recommended that I should return to work fulltime. "Pull yourself up by your bootstraps, and be strong," she added. "Show them you can take it."

I tried to explain to her that I was on part-time maternity leave because Vanessa was just over a year old. There was no way I could have coped with fulltime work at that stage; it was all I could do to keep going as I was. I felt she didn't understand that I was at breaking point, but I told her I would go away and think about it.

On 13 September I applied for a transfer to the EEO Unit. There was only one other applicant, a young man who had been in the service for only three years and was in his first year of study. He got the job. In October I volunteered to be a member of a working party set up to examine issues relating to part-time work and the NSW Police Services policies on pregnancy and maternity leave. I applied unsuccessfully for further transfers and did other courses. Eventually I was transferred to the Strategy and Review Section within the Establishment Control Branch, where job descriptions were written; I had already done some of this work. But once again I was given menial tasks.

I didn't want the bastards to beat me, but the depression and anxiety were awful. I was having trouble dragging myself out of bed in the morning, knowing I would be facing hours of boredom at a desk. As well as being an alcoholic I am a workaholic, and this was the worst punishment they could have given me.

In February 1994 I applied to be the head teacher on the Initial Response Officers Course. Buying a new outfit for the interview, I had high hopes this time I would establish a new career path. The interview, with Detective Inspector Matthew Casey, went for about an hour. The work involved regular travelling to Goulburn, which would have been difficult as Vanessa was only a baby, but I decided it would be a new start. Unfortunately the office was right next door to the old Fraud Squad, so I would have had to constantly walk past the very people I'd complained about. But I thought I could be strong enough to cope with that. It was all going well; they seemed keen to have me.

Then at the end of the interview Casey said, "Bill Gould will probably be coming over to do the detective notes."

I was wary. "In that case, I'll have think about whether I can accept the position or not," I said. I was apprehensive about what Gould might do to me, given the opportunity.

That night Claudia Campanelli called to tell me, "People at the Fraud Squad know of your application and said, 'You had better not even consider it.'"

So that was that. I kept trying, applying for other positions, looking for every avenue to revive my career. But word had gone around. At one interview the guy looked at me and said, "Don't clean out your locker."

I was asked whether I wanted to come under the new police Internal Informers policy. I would be one of the first officers in the scheme. According to the rules I was allowed a case officer and a mentor but, disillusioned with the Police Force, I at first said 'no' to both. I later thought I had better change my mind and called Fitzpatrick. He then said I had been refused permission to go on this, as I had rejected the offer. After several more telephone conversations, however, I was placed on the scheme. Fitzpatrick told me my case officer was to be Sergeant John Cameron and my mentor Chief Superintendent Reginald White.

Neither of them seemed to know what they were supposed to do, and I certainly didn't. On 12 January 1994 I asked White what was happening. He read through the booklet with me. "Any problems?" he asked.

"I keep hearing that I'm a bitch, I'm after compensation and then I'm going to resign," I told him.

"Look, this is only a short part of your career. In Detectives, other people get harassed, non-drinkers, ethnics. If I can be any help, my door is always open." Dumbfounded, I walked out of his office.

A few days later, having been with the Establishment Control Branch for about six months, I left work on stress leave, unable to take it any more. They had cracked me. I was so lucky, however, that I had Greg's love and support and my darling Vanessa. Looking into her beautiful face I knew I had to stay alive: she needed her mum so much.

Meanwhile, things were not looking good for Jamison and the others in the Fraud Squad. On secondment to the National Crime Authority, Harry Neyenhuys had compiled a report on the section late in 1992, which had been instrumental in closing it and forming the new Fraud Enforcement Agency late in 1993. While things were collapsing around him, Jamison apparently said, "We are a sinking ship and if we stick together we will be all right . . . Debbie has done us a lot of damage, but we can ride this out."

Several people told me that if any of the staff were interviewed by Internal Affairs, Jamison would wait for them in the kitchen afterwards and go through their statements with them. Apparently this involved an endless stream of people. He also conducted squad meetings. Only about five officers did not go and show their statements to Jamison, including Greg, Bruce Van Der Graff, Harry Neyenhuys and Claudia Campanelli. Young Steven Williams, who was used as a typist, driver and general fall guy, was a wild card. He admitted a lot of things that were going on. Perhaps he had a moment of clarity and saw some of the truth, or they had just caught him on a day when he didn't have his wits about him. A few of the younger cops let things slip due to their inexperience.

Jamison focused on the other woman in the section to give him support. By the time the Fraud Squad was about to crash down on them, the number of women had increased and the new permanent women attached to the section were Sue Newcombe, Helen Gilbert and Sue Vine. None of them supported me. I hope someone does a study sometime showing why women don't stick together in a male-dominated environment.

Jamison was intelligent enough to realise that this was the end of the Fraud Squad as it had always been run. In the end everyone was left to sink or swim and find their own place to go. Only three people were offered a job at the Fraud Enforcement Agency, one of those being Greg. Jamison wasn't asked to stay on. It must have been a bitter pill for him to swallow going back to duties in uniform.

An anonymous complaint was lodged with Internal Affairs in early 1994, alleging that Harry Neyenhuys and I had made a false travelling allowance claim in 1990. We had arrived in Perth for a fraud investigation as part of a brief for Nelson Chad that had to be done quickly, and found that the accommodation for the trip had been booked and paid for by the insurance company that was the subject of the investigation. I wasn't sure about the procedure for repaying them, but when we came back to Sydney Neyenhuys told me the company's solicitor had said we did not need to. We checked with Jamison, who told us that as long as we filled in an expenses claim, for food and other costs, that was OK. I typed the claim form out myself – it was standard procedure – and my claim form had been signed and certified by Rome Martin. I later heard a whisper that an officer had pulled the complaint off Jamison's office computer late one night.

After giving information to Internal Affairs, I was always worried that someone in the Fraud Squad would find something to cook up against me. In the end an old travelling allowance allegation turned out to be their best effort. They had it in for Harry Neyenhuys because of his report recommending the closure of the Fraud Squad. Jamison wasn't giving up without a fight, however. When being interviewed by Internal Affairs about mismanagement and corruption, he told them that Harry and I were both Dutch and members of some fundamentalist church group. Wrong on both accounts.

In early 1994 I rang to ask what was happening about the investigation into Parramatta Detectives and the statement I had given. According to my notes Jim Marowitz had been found guilty of corruption and given a bond. Ron Marowitz was in trouble over another matter, but was not prosecuted, and resigned. My informant also told me that he had been directed not to take any action in relation to the break and enter incident, as Ron had already been charged over something else, and there was therefore no point in chasing him over this as well.

On 4 February 1994, I finally chucked in the towel. Images of senior detectives from the Fraud Squad yelling at me or looking through the windows haunted my thoughts. Fear of being alone was joined by dread of going down the street; even pushing Vanessa through Balmain's streets and parks in her pram, which I had loved doing, became too difficult. My doctor had put me on Prozac, and I lay on the lounge and stared at the ceiling for much of the day while Vanessa played on the floor beside me. I don't recall important parts of Vanessa's early life through being so traumatised, and I feel I was robbed of a very important period of her development. Other people didn't understand what we were going through. Greg tried as best he could to keep his little family together.

On 2 March I tried to ring Fitzpatrick as I had heard nothing from the Police Service about the new police informers program. I wanted to know what was happening and where I stood. I was told that the investigation of the Fraud Squad would be finished in early April and that Chief Superintendent Reginald White, my designated mentor, would call me back. The following day John Cameron, my case officer, did call me and said that the Fraud Squad matter should be finished on the twenty-first. He also apologised for not being in touch.

Around this time I joined Whistleblowers Australia. It was a higher power that sent me to Dr Jean Lennane, the national president, who is also a wonderful doctor. She was exactly the right person for me at that time. Until I joined Whistleblowers, I was convinced I was the one who had been in the wrong. But group support showed me that other people in large bureaucracies who stand up to senior management when they see corruption also have a job done on them. My story is not unique. Like me, other members of the group were told they had ruined their careers because of their big mouths, that the price they paid has been too high and they should have just kept quiet, as others would have done. But I cannot be like that, and neither can other members of the group.

Whistleblowers Australia have given me support, encouragement and hope, showing me that the behaviour I encountered through speaking out about corruption was typical. In my time there I have heard many horror stories. My shame at what had happened to my career lessened slightly, and I felt vindicated in my decision, which was also Greg's, not to run and hide, no matter what happened. At one point management committee meetings were held in our lounge room. People were passionate about their cases and there were many heated discussions, with which I sympathised and which I understood. At last I wasn't isolated, I felt I belonged somewhere again.

On 11 March 1994, after a conversation with Kim Cook, I made one of the most important decisions of my life. Greg and I met Kim in a house at Leichhardt for a secret meeting with the independent New South Wales state politician John Hatton. Hatton was a wiry little bloke in a grey suit, whose face bore the lines gained from years of fighting corruption, but at the same time displayed genuine warmth. Also present was a newspaper reporter, Morgan Ogg, a young man with frizzy dark hair in a ponytail. He had been working with Hatton, but wouldn't have looked out of place as an undercover police operative.

"I need what you have on the Police Force," Hatton explained. "To get the truth out about police corruption." For more than twenty years he had been working to force a Royal Commission into the New South Wales Police. He had an aura of strength and integrity and I knew immediately I could trust him. His proposal frightened me, however, because I had Greg and Vanessa to think of. What if something happened to me, what if the cops tried to shut me up for good? I already knew what it felt like to be an outsider in my job; it was quite different to go outside the Police Force and to be placing all my faith in one lean politician and a young crime reporter. Greg and I felt like moles working against our organisation. Although we knew what we were doing was right, our conditioning in police culture still made us both feel uncomfortable.

Meanwhile, the investigation into my travel allowance claim was going ahead. On 22 April Greg and I met with Nancy Hendley, a legal adviser at the Police Association. Then we all went to Police Headquarters to have a meeting with the then Assistant Commissioner of Professional Responsibility, Jeffrey Jarratt, and Detective Superintendent Geoffrey Schuberg, the Commander of Internal Affairs. I wanted to tape the whole of our conversation but they refused. The only compromise they would give was for Nancy to be present to take minutes.

I tried to hand Jarratt a copy of the complaint against Neyenhuys and me and made it very clear to Jarratt that Jamison had in fact approved our claim.

"I know about the complaint," Jarratt replied. "But even if the DPP say you are to be charged, the decision is up to me." He left the meeting and Assistant Commissioner Geoff Schuberg, the then commander of Internal Affairs, came in. I tried to hand him a copy of Jamison's complaint.

"I already have a copy ... I can't believe they were stupid enough to do this." I told him the background, including Jamison's approval of our TA.

"We can give you a job at IA tomorrow."

"Nancy, put that down," I told her. "I'd come back off sick report tomorrow if I could have a job at IA."

Schuberg said I could have a job in the Customer Service Section of IA for twelve months. I knew that this was a new task force for members of the public who could call to make comments or lodge complaints. People doing these jobs had a monthly counselling session from Welfare, as they had to deal with so many irate customers. I thought it would all be too much for me, being on Prozac as I was. Besides, it was a uniform job.

"Why can't I come to IA as an investigator?" I asked. "There are no women attached to IA at the moment and no one is being trained to take complaints about EEO issues." I didn't want to go back to a situation where I was isolated from the whole Police Service.

"I can't have you at IA at the moment because they're investigating the TA complaint lodged against you. There are a lot of people at IA who were friendly with the officers you have complained about." End of story.

After the meeting I kept asking Nancy Hendley for a copy of the notes she had taken in shorthand, but I did not receive them until four months later, and they were just over two pages long. The meeting lasted for two and a half hours, and in my opinion the notes do not fully record what was said.

On Tuesday 31 May Sergeant Phil Neave interviewed me about the trip to Perth that was the subject of the TA claim. Harry Neyenhuys had already given them a full statement and urged me to do the same, saying he had been told that if I did, the whole thing would be written off. But my legal advice was that, if I was criminally cautioned (as I probably would be) I should say nothing, and I was going to go with that. Harry was very angry.

I had my case officer Sergeant John Cameron come to the interview as a support person and when we went into the interview room I told Neave I wanted the interview recorded on ERISP recording equipment. He said he didn't think it was necessary, and I picked up the phone and asked to be put through to Jarratt's office. After about an hour and a half and much coming and going, a fuming Neave brought the ERISP equipment into the interview room.

Once the equipment had been turned on, Neave issued me with the official criminal caution. Neyenhuys and I were the only ones from the Fraud Squad who were criminally cautioned by IA when interviewed. Everyone else had been interviewed departmentally. Because a caution was administered, there was a possibility of criminal charges, and on my solicitor's advice I said, "I've got nothing to add at this stage." If the investigation had just been departmental they could have directed me to answer and I would have had to comply. Neave never contacted me again about giving a statement.

Early in June I had a meeting with Assistant Commissioner Christine Nixon, who told me she would try and find somewhere for me to go back to work. About three weeks later she suggested I ring Ken Moroney at the Police Advisory Centre about possible employment on a task force looking into some police shootings in Victoria. I contacted Moroney's office and left a message, but had no reply; the same thing happened when I called a week later. I didn't pursue the matter further as my health had gone downhill again and I was prescribed further medication, with my doctor saying I was not well enough to return to work at that stage anyway.

I heard nothing further about the TA allowance matter until 20 October when Cameron called to tell me that the DPP had not recommended any criminal charges against Neyenhuys and me. Internal Affairs had not told me the outcome of Neave's investigation. On 17 January 1995 Chief Inspector Lola Scott told Greg that there were to be no departmental charges against me, but I was not officially informed of this at the time. At different times over these months I asked Greg and Cameron to request that the Police Service put in writing that no criminal or departmental charges would be laid against me, but apparently they were told that it was up to the ombudsman's office to advise me.

On 21 January 1995 John Hutchings from the ombudsman's office rang Greg to advise that there were to be no departmental charges. Several months later I finally received a letter confirming this.

These days, there is a Public Disclosure Act that allows for criminal charges to be laid against anyone who makes a payback complaint against whistleblowers. So perhaps it will be easier for future whistleblowers to speak out.

While I was working at the Establishment Control Branch, I talked to Christine Nixon about the harassment I had suffered at the Fraud Squad, and she advised me to lodge a complaint with the Anti-Discrimination Board. She told me that one of her closest friends in the police had just gone under and left, due to years of harassment, and that she herself was sick of seeing women leave because of the bloody stupidity of men. She had recommended to a number of female officers that they lodge a complaint, but she said it took real guts to go through with it. Such a radical thought had never crossed my mind. Christine was immensely supportive to me, and she inspired me to lodge an anti-discrimination claim.

The matter dragged on for months but finally a conciliation conference was held on 8 November 1994. Christine Nixon, representing the police, told the conciliator, Christine Sultana of the Anti-Discrimination Board, that to improve the handling of future complaints about sexual harassment, ERISP audio recording equipment would be used in all IA interviews. Not only that, but officers trained in EEO issues would be appointed to the Internal Affairs section.

It was a great loss to New South Wales when Christine left and became Commissioner of the Victorian Police Force. I felt a bit like the sacrificial lamb, but I believed I helped make it easier for other women who come after me. Yet I am still hearing about typewritten interviews.

At this conference a solicitor from the Redfern Legal Centre represented me, making certain claims on my behalf. Nixon said she would get back to me about those by late in November, but she wrote to my solicitor midway through the following year, in July 1995, saying she could not proceed with conciliation while the investigation into the Fraud Squad was continuing.

A handful of brave policemen supplied statutory declarations supporting my claims of what had happened at the Fraud Squad. Sadly, Claudia Campanelli was the only woman who supported my complaints of sexual harassment and being discriminated against on the grounds of pregnancy. The other three women at the section were not going to get involved, even though they had complained to me about some of the things that had been said and done to them.

I travelled down to Canberra to get Claudia's statement, and was shocked to see her. This bright, bubbly girl had become a closed-down, frumpy woman who looked much older than her actual age, living in an old fibro cottage on the outskirts of the city. Claudia had lost her faith in humans after her trauma in the police force and was now surrounded by animals. Three cats and two dogs were living in the house. She also had goldfish floating on top of the water in their tank, and a chook. Claudia and I had drifted further and further apart as she remained in the horror of her past life in the Fraud Squad. I had to fight depression too, but going under was not an option for me. I had a family to live for; Greg and Vanessa were my reason to keep going.

I finally had my conciliation hearing at the Equal Opportunity Commission on 18 March 1996. It brought up many of the bad things that had happened to me in the job, but even then I was too scared to mention everything and everybody for fear of retaliation. I'm a lot braver these days. I won compensation. It was a victory, yet they could never pay me enough money to compensate me for what I have been through. You can't put a monetary value on being frightened for your life or on the loss of a daughter. I also received a letter of apology which I had asked to be signed by the commissioner, Tony Lauer, but it came back signed by Christine Nixon.

When I joined the NSW Police Service in 1984 I had no major health problems, and continued to have none during my first five years of service. But from 4 February 1994 I was on sick report suffering from anxiety, depression and illness due to work-related harassment and stress. I had seen two psychiatrists because of the effect of my work environment on me. On 7 March 1994 I applied to have my absence since February 1994 designated as 'Hurt on Duty'; in effect I was applying for a medical discharge.

One of the hardest decisions I ever had to make was to apply to leave the cops. It felt like a knife in my chest. I had loved my job, breathed it, but it was killing me. My biological family had rejected me; now the same thing had happened with my police family.

In July I was asked to see a psychiatrist in Hurstville to be assessed about my Hurt on Duty application. I wrote to Christine Nixon objecting to having to attend a doctor appointed by the Police Service. Her reply was basically: "If you want a pension, you will have to go and see our doctor."

I saw this psychiatrist on no fewer than seven different occasions. He was a hard old man who kept trying to catch me out, and had a reputation for knocking back pension applications. He kept trying to make out it wasn't all that bad. I kept breaking down and crying.

In the end, the doctor recommended that I apply to be discharged as medically unfit due to stress and that the stress should be classified as Hurt on Duty. I wasn't sure what to do next: should I apply for a medical discharge, or would it go through automatically? The original Hurt on Duty application was also still to be officially decided; should I wait for that before applying to be discharged?

Greg made many enquiries on my behalf, trying to find out why the determination of the original application for HOD was taking so long. I came to believe that the delay was deliberate because I was a whistleblower. But on 23 February 1995 I was told that the decision had been delayed while they finalised the inquiry into some of the Fraud Squad matters I had raised, and they were still waiting on the outcome of the Internal Affairs investigation into the TA claim allegations against Neyenhuys and myself.

Finally, in January 1996, the day after a confrontation with Lauer at a public meeting at Balmain at which members of the press were present, I was told that my HOD claim had been approved as from 11 January and that I was now entitled to a Police Service pension. This was a relief financially, but I was still grieving. All I had ever wanted to do was be a cop. I felt very hurt and angry that the opportunity to have a long-term career in the service had been taken from me. I still do. It's hard not being a cop any more.

It was even harder being the wife of a cop. Greg still had his job, and it hurt that he was working with some of my former colleagues. He would go on trips for a week or two at a time and ring me at home, where I was up to my armpits in dirty nappies. It was very depressing.

CHAPTER 18

THE ROYAL COMMISSION

By early 1994 John Hatton's attempts to have a Royal Commission into the New South Wales Police Service were intensifying. The Liberals under Premier John Fahey were a minority government in New South Wales, and he knew that if the three independent MPs added their numbers to the Labor opposition and all supported a Royal Commission, it stood a good chance of getting through.

Hatton had been waiting for this delicate balance for almost all of his political life; he knew this was about the only chance that he as an independent MP would have to influence the direction of parliament. He already had willing supporters for a wide-ranging and thorough investigation of the upper ranks of the Police Service in the other independent MPs, Clover Moore and Dr Peter Macdonald. His greatest problem was gaining the support of the opposition Labor Party, led by Bob Carr. The ALP, it seemed, was reluctant to open up this particular can of worms. At the same time, Labor was pressuring the independents to lend their support to a censure motion against Terry Griffiths, the then police minister. Hatton rejected this, as he felt it fell far short of what was needed. He expressed his exasperation to our small group of supporters and kept us informed on a regular basis.

It was now early May 1994, and the chances of Labor winning the approaching state election were not looking good. Bob Carr and his team therefore had nothing to lose in giving Hatton what he wanted. Things started to happen very quickly. I had already provided Hatton with about fifteen statutory declarations detailing my knowledge and experience of corruption, mismanagement and sexual harassment during my police career.

On a Sunday evening Hatton called me at home. He told me, "I have spoken to the Labor Party and they have consented to support my motion for the Royal Commission. I will be making my speech to parliament this week."

"Have you got enough police to support you yet?"

"I have enough, but much of it is not as current as your evidence. I'd really like you and Greg to be in the public gallery to support me."

"After all this, of course we'll be there," I said.

On the afternoon of Wednesday 11 May 1994 I made my way from Balmain to Parliament House, Macquarie Street, Sydney. Greg met me on the steps after coming straight from the office. This was the start of a long evening. Greg and I had dinner with John Hatton in the parliamentary dining room.

Hatton was both nervous and excited, rather like an athlete before a major race.

His speech to parliament lasted about eighty minutes. He asserted that corruption was entrenched in the senior levels of the NSW Police Service, that Internal Affairs was corrupt and that senior officers closed ranks to cover up corrupt activity. He raised concerns about the competence of senior police including Commissioner Tony Lauer, Assistant Commissioner Norm Moroney, former Assistant Commissioner Col Cole and Superintendent Bob Myatt. He detailed information about a police officer being told to carry out surveillance on a former attorney-general, Frank Walker. A significant portion of the speech covered the information I supplied: corruption at Parramatta Detectives, the leaking of information by internal investigating police, Tony Lauer's calling me a whistleblower and an outcast, corruption, death threats and sexual harassment at the Fraud Squad and leaks with cover-ups by the Professional Integrity Branch.

It was hard going, sitting in the public gallery and hearing my working life discussed so critically. As the evening rolled along, the gallery began to fill with familiar not-so-friendly faces; word about the debate had spread and Lauer had rallied many of his senior troops to show support for the police minister. Some wore suits, many were in uniform. But Hatton and his supporters refused to be intimidated.

The debate that followed Hatton's speech was passionate and lasted for hours, well into the night. But finally in the early hours of the morning a vote was taken and John Fahey announced that a Royal Commission into police corruption was to be established. I was stunned when he apologised publicly for the way Kim Cook and I had been treated. We were so elated: Hatton had won!

I should have been prepared for what was to follow, but I wasn't. The media attention was huge, with front-page headlines; it was the top story on the TV and radio news. In some circles Hatton was being lauded as a knight in shining armour; his critics dammed him as a zealot and troublemaker. My name was mentioned in most of the papers and there was a photograph in the *Sydney Morning Herald*. In a press conference Tony Lauer said, when asked about his apparent lack of support for police whistleblowers, "I don't ever claim to be perfect; I have on occasion crossed the road against the 'don't walk' light."

When the Commission started, the TV viewing public was entertained by fantastic footage of police taking money. We saw scenes of corrupt police caught on film with their pants down, some literally. Who could forget Graham 'Chook' Fowler's famous words after he sat blankly in the box watching money changing hands in the front seat of a car: "That's not me, it must be an actor"?

But I was too traumatised really to enjoy all this, or to feel any satisfaction because of it. I had a black cloud hanging over my head. All my former colleagues in the Police Force knew what I had done. Every night my disturbed sleep was filled with dark figures grabbing me, shooting me, smothering me slowly. Every time the phone rang I would jump, hoping and again dreading that it could be the Royal Commission wanting me to give evidence immediately. I was going to lots of AA meetings.

The boys made Greg's life at work impossible. Luckily a senior officer felt sorry for him and gave him work at a task force away from them. Unfortunately even then he wasn't safe. He had put his name down to play at a police golf function and was told that nobody would play with him. It was horrible for him, and he felt as if he'd had enough. He had a wife who was not functioning, was trapped in a small task force with his career in tatters and everyone was angry with him. Colleagues past and present would walk past him saying, "Can't you control your bloody wife?"

Vanessa was four years old now, and we had been trying to have another child for some time. Greg and I were both brought up as only children, and this was something I did not wish upon our daughter. Our doctor had said that we would never be able to have children and I was starting to believe that maybe Vanessa had been a fluke. So we began the long journey of IVF. Greg's sperm count was low and the ectopic pregnancy of years before had left me with only one fallopian tube, so we thought it was time for a bit of intervention.

Greg was fantastic when I had a laparoscopy to see if my tube was blocked; when I regained consciousness there he was, holding beautiful long-stemmed yellow roses. Six weeks later we had an appointment about the IVF procedure. As we sat on the beautiful leather lounge chairs in the waiting room I said to Greg, "I feel really crook, like I'm pregnant." He told me I had pregnancy on the brain. On the way home I made him stop at a chemist and buy a pregnancy kit. I was right.

This pregnancy was much like mine with Vanessa. I was green and throwing up the whole time. I should have been thrilled, but I wasn't. Not this time. So much had happened: my career had fallen to bits, at that stage I didn't know whether I was facing criminal charges about the travel allowance business, and I was dreading giving evidence in front of the Royal Commission.

At ten weeks I had an ultrasound. The female technician said, "Looks like twins to me." We were so excited. But soon afterwards I started bleeding and Greg rushed me to the hospital. Our obstetrician examined me and said, "Sorry Deb, it sounds like you're having a miscarriage. This doesn't mean there won't be more children."

At a later ultrasound I found I had lost one baby, but the other was hanging in there. Although I felt like an emotional wreck, I tried to lie down and rest as much as I could. This was difficult; not only did I have Vanessa to look after, but we were fostering Corey, another four-year-old who was a member of my family, through the Department of Community Services. At the time it was not appropriate for him to be with his natural mother. We loved him dearly, but he had emotional problems and was a handful.

I had made it to twenty-five weeks when I received the phone call I had been dreading from the Royal Commission: "OK Debbie, you're on next. Wood has so much work that we are bringing in another judge. You will be the first cab off the rank with Judge Urquhart." I said I was ill but nobody seemed particularly interested in my physical condition, though they promised me I would only be two days in the witness box. I thought, *OK, let's do this and get it over and done with so I can just focus on the pregnancy.*

Turning up at the Commission that first morning, on 7 May 1996, was nerve-wracking. I didn't know what I was going to say, not having seen the statement I had made for nearly a year. It was over a hundred pages long. Virginia Bell, counsel assisting, led me through my statement for two days as I gave my evidence-in-chief. I was not prepared for what happened next. One by one, each of the other barristers cross-examined me about my entire career, starting at the Police Academy. When one had finished, the next one would stand and start back at the beginning. I felt as if I was answering the same questions over and over again, that they were trying to discredit me. Every time my barrister objected, she would be shut down to the point where she just gave up. Because I was the bloody whistleblower who had supported John Hatton and assisted him in getting the Royal Commission, I was the one on trial. This was not what I had expected from seeing the way Justice Wood had protected other Commission witnesses, but of course they hadn't been whistleblowers. Maybe that was why this segment of the Royal Commission was being conducted so differently from those preceding it.

As well as being ill with the pregnancy, I had the flu. I could not stop coughing and was chilled to the bone with a fever. Justice Urquhart kept interrupting proceedings as I was coughing so much. I would then go out to the toilets and have a good cough and sometimes even vomit. One of the newspaper articles at the time referred to all the drinks and cough medicines I had in the box with me.

On the fourth day in the box – so much for being told it would be a two-day examination – I had to leave due to my coughing. I went into the toilets as usual, and I felt a popping sensation in my cervix. I ignored it, as I was trying to focus on the next attack on my credibility. By this stage in my pregnancy I was wearing a pad and later I was told that what I had thought was urine – I thought I was wetting myself with all this coughing – was in fact amniotic fluid. My water had broken.

The cross-examination about my character went on for a further two days. This was now my sixth day in the box. As we stopped for the lunch break four more barristers representing people I had named stood up and sought leave to cross-examine me. Urquhart granted their requests. Greg and I went to an Italian restaurant around the corner for lunch. I put my head down on the table and sobbed, "I am so sick, I can't do this any more." And then I realised something else: I had not felt the baby move for a long time.

As the Commission hearing was about to resume I marched up to Virginia Bell. "I can't believe how you people have treated me," I told her. "This is the thanks I get for putting myself and my family on the line. I'm off to see a doctor right now. My baby has not moved for days. I shouldn't be here. You knew this was never going to end." I stormed out of the courtroom.

I never heard any more from the Royal Commission. I was so disillusioned. I had fought so hard to support John Hatton, done my best to give evidence to the Commission, and they still used me so badly. Unfortunately for me, my psychiatrist was overseas at the time. Poor old Greg was the only one in my corner and, being due to give evidence when I had finished, he was under a lot of pressure as well.

Too ill to even get myself to a doctor for medical treatment, all I could do was fall into bed. The next day I was still coughing and spluttering, still alternately burning and shivering. I thought everything would be all right if I rested, and that the only thing wrong with me was stress and a dose of the flu.

The cleaner was downstairs the following day and I lay there in bed listening to her vacuum the floors. Corey and Vanessa were at their pre-school. All of a sudden I became aware of light contractions. A couple of hours later I realised that they were coming and going. I looked at the bedroom clock and noted the time. Three minutes later they started again. Three minutes after that the contractions were back again. I couldn't believe it. I realised I must be in labour, but I was only twenty-six weeks pregnant, and still had fourteen weeks to go. I went into shock. All I could say was, "No, not my baby."

With tears running down my face, I tried to ring Greg. His mobile was turned off as he was just about to get in the box to give evidence. I called the office of the Royal Commission, telling them to send Greg to the hospital. I was in labour.

Not thinking straight, I grabbed my purse and ran down the stairs. Instead of calling an ambulance I jumped into our big silver Nissan Patrol and headed off down the road. Crossing the Harbour Bridge heading for the Mater hospital I almost smashed into oncoming traffic during a contraction. Crying at the same time didn't make driving any easier.

Pulling up at the entrance of the hospital I ran in yelling, "Help me quick, my baby's coming. Stop it! You have to stop it!"

I was wheeled up to the labour ward, where a young doctor told me, "I'm sorry, we can't help you here. We are a private hospital, we can't handle premature births. I have called an ambulance, we are going to send you over to the Royal North Shore hospital."

I was rushed to the Royal North Shore, where Greg met me. They gave me a steroid injection to help mature the baby's lungs and placed me on a Ventolin drip to try and stop the contractions. A wonderful nurse supported me through that night. Even after I threw up all over her she kept smiling. Greg went quiet. Fear was etched upon his face as he sat holding my hand. We were told that I needed to keep the baby inside at least another twenty-four hours so they could give me another steroid injection. This would give the baby the best chance of survival.

But the contractions just wouldn't stop. After eighteen hours I heard the worst news. "I'm sorry, the baby is coming now," said Dr Hartman. "It's not good."

Hayes was born not long after. He entered the world as a tiny non-breathing being: Greg cut the umbilical cord. The baby was taken away and put on life support straight away. Greg was torn as to whether to stay with me or go to his son.

The doctor tried to pull out the placenta by the umbilical cord, but the cord broke. "That can't be good," I said.

"No it's not, but you're so early that this can happen."

The placenta, which had broken into pieces, had to be removed and I was taken down to the operating theatre to face more surgery. After an epidural and a long battle over the fact that I still had total feeling, I was finally put under. They gave me a lot of medication but I was so wired that they had little effect. Halfway through the procedure I sat up on the operating table, startling everyone in the theatre. I was soon under again.

When I came to I felt like death. Ivan Ransom, the minister from the Presbyterian church in Balmain, arrived with his wife Joan after Greg had called him to let him know what had happened. He conducted an emergency christening as we did not expect Hayes to live long. He weighed only 1100 grams and had so little body fat that you could almost see through him. His skin had a yellowish tinge and was covered in hair. Wires were hooked up to him everywhere.

But, incredibly, Hayes survived. I felt absolutely dreadful for days, however. A couple of days later a team of doctors came to my room to tell me that I was so rundown from the flu that the infection had crossed over to my blood and I now had blood poisoning. No wonder I was feeling so terrible. This was not good for Hayes; he also had blood poisoning and jaundice.

After ten days I was told they needed my bed and I would have to leave the hospital without my son. I had to take drugs to make milk as I had given birth too early in my pregnancy to lactate. Now I had to go to the hospital every day with the expressed milk which needed to be collected every four hours. It was so hard not to have my baby.

We still had Vanessa and Corey to take care of, and Greg took time off work to help me. Hayes stayed in hospital for three months. Every time I drove up to the hospital gates with the milk I felt as if there was a rock in the pit of my stomach. I knew that if a child was very ill or had died, the hospital would not call if they knew you were due to come in. I got to know five different families whose babies were next to Hayes' incubator and they had all passed away. I never knew whether Hayes would be next. Greg and I lived on McDonalds and pizza during this time and we both stacked on weight. We were both too stressed and exhausted to cook real food.

We took Hayes home attached to a monitor to control his breathing; he had a tendency to stop breathing if left to himself. We had a lot of pressure from every direction. Greg's parents did not help, and we had problems with Corey. His mother was on methadone and every time she had a supervised access visit with him, he would come back very upset and it would take days to settle him down again. After one visit he said, "You and Greg are bad people, you put bad people in gaol. Bad people are my friends. You make my mummy very sad." We never even received a thank you for the two years he was with us. This was when I cut all ties with every member of my family.

Not long after Hayes was home I was down at Balmain shops. I saw a mate, Clayton, in the street, who commented, "You don't look well. I hope you're not pregnant?". Suddenly the penny dropped. I rushed into the local GP and took a pregnancy test.

The blood drained from Greg's face when I showed him the familiar white plastic tube with the pink indicator. This pregnancy was like the other two, I spent a lot of time throwing up. At twenty-five weeks I started bleeding. "What if I have another premature birth?" I asked Greg.

Within hours I was back at the Mater hospital. "I can't do this again," I said, tears rolling down my cheeks. My ever-kind paediatrician looked at me with sad eyes. "I'm sorry, Deb, there are no incubated beds in Sydney. We are working out arrangements to fly you to Melbourne or Newcastle." At the last minute an incubator became available at King George V hospital. I was off in the ambulance again.

I was given injections for the baby's lungs. They did an ultrasound and even though they would not tell me the result, I knew my baby was a little girl. Greg sat on my bed all night and we went through possible names. I was losing lots of water and knew it would not be long before I gave birth. We decided on Bronte, named after the suburb of Sydney that was our special place, and Irene after my mother. I sent Greg home in the morning to have a shower and get some sleep.

Less than an hour later I was on the floor having a seizure. A doctor was rushed in. "You have an infection," he told me. "We cannot find a heartbeat for the baby." I went into surgery for an emergency caesarean. The doctor said he did not know if we would find the baby alive.

When they opened me up they discovered that my uterus was so badly infected that Bronte was covered in pus. She weighed even less than Hayes, only 800 grams and, like him, they did not know whether she would survive. She remained on life support for eighteen days, as he had done.

One afternoon I was sitting by her bed, feeling desperately unhappy. Bronte was so tiny and fragile, really struggling to breathe on life support, and still coughing up phlegm. I couldn't even touch her, just look at her through the glass of the incubator. Greg was at work and unable to be contacted. I will never forget how I felt as I cried on the balcony of the hospital. I was alone, waiting for my baby to die.

One thing that helped me through this period was going to meetings of Alcoholics Anonymous. It was enough just to keep my sanity; the drug I was taking was a depressant. But I couldn't afford to be depressed because I had to express milk for Bronte, as I had with Hayes. I couldn't have kept going without Greg pushing me. "Think of Bronte, you just have to get out of bed and express again," he would say. "She needs all the help you can give. This is your most important job at the moment."

I lived the AA slogan 'a day at a time'. I had to keep in the present. I couldn't dwell on the past and wrongs done or what the future would hold. Bronte's condition went up and down almost daily. Her up days were still pretty down compared to the other babies. At one stage they were even contemplating a heart operation. I thought things could not get any worse. There was a constant worry about brain bleeds, eyes and hearing. All things that coincide with prematurity.

It was four months before Bronte came off oxygen and left the hospital. I was told there were to be no more babies. I still pinch myself that she survived at twenty-five weeks. There are not many walking around as good as her. We count ourselves blessed that we have three beautiful children after being told we would never have any.

But life was very tough. It had been a hard year, with the Royal Commission and two premature births; Bronte was born only eight months after Hayes should have been. Corey had gone to live with his biological family, but I struggled with the two little babies. Greg was very ill also; all the stress had caught up with him. His work environment was still very hostile, which did not help his condition of post-traumatic stress. He got to the point where he was unable to work. He used up all his sick days, holidays and long service leave. But he had nowhere to go when he did return to work.

During this time we received no support from our police friends or our biological family. This was a very dark and lonely time for us both; Greg and I put our heads down and lived life day by day.

Then one day Michael Drury was walking through Pitt Street and bumped into Greg. Over coffee, Greg poured out all that had happened. Michael immediately offered him a position in the Drug Enforcement Agency (now known as the Drug Squad). Greg was apprehensive about returning to work. He wanted to protect his family and believed he had a better chance of doing so if he remained inside the force. At the DEA he worked hard and benefited from having little contact with mainstream police, yet he was still marked as a whistleblower. He was treated with suspicion from afar by fellow workers. Eventually he moved into a small team of a few detectives who investigated clandestine drug laboratories. This was very dangerous and tedious work that few others in the Drug Squad were interested in.

CHAPTER 19

A WHOLE NEW WORLD

Hayes turned out to be blond and very cute. I thought he was very advanced. He didn't bother with crawling; at eleven months he pulled himself up on a chair and started running. He was also very conscious of smell and noise. At this time we decided to take him to see a bowel surgeon as he did not go to the toilet very often, sometimes not for days on end. We were told that we had nothing to worry about. He was a normal child.

Hayes was very active and I had to watch him like a hawk. Our terrace house in Balmain was really getting me down too. There were steep stairs, and I had to take the kids to a park every day to get them out of the cramped conditions. The place was just too small for us now. Greg was very reluctant to leave Balmain, but the kids needed a real backyard.

The women at the baby health centre could see I was exhausted and they arranged for me to go on the Home Start program. I was very grateful for the support and friendship of Jenny Reid, who came around every week to put on a load of washing and watch the kids while I got a couple of hours' sleep. She would even pack us into the car and take us all to the beach.

One day Hayes was running on the sand naked. I saw him standing behind a couple sitting on a blanket kissing. They had a beautiful cane basket open with champagne glasses and chicken. I couldn't work out why Hayes was standing there, then to my horror I saw that he was weeing all over their lunch. Swooping down I grabbed him and made a hasty exit. He grew more and more unpredictable. He would jump and climb on all the furniture. I was told not to worry; he was 'just a boy'. He certainly was nothing like Vanessa had been; for one thing, he could be violent and destructive.

Meanwhile, I had succeeded in making Greg agree that we should move, and we had found our dream home in Croydon, an inner western suburb of Sydney. One bit of luck had been the explosion of the real estate market; the prices of homes in Balmain had doubled in five years, enabling us to buy a real house with a pool. It was a far cry from the poverty I had grown up in. I was a bit lost when we first moved, but my weekly visit from Jenny kept me going. Greg and I missed Balmain, but not as much as Hayes did. The change really upset him.

Everybody in the family, it seemed, had problems of some sort. Vanessa, who had started kindergarten, was bleeding from the bowel and underwent a general anaesthetic at the age of five. It was discovered that she had a heart murmur, too.

Because of all this, and a high lead content in her blood from living in the inner city, she had dark circles under her eyes, and had no energy. Bronte needed daily antibiotics for her first four years of life due to problems with kidney reflux. Greg and I were not well and under enormous pressure. The early days at Croydon seemed like a blur as we dragged ourselves through every day as best we could.

When Hayes lost all his normal language almost overnight, alarm bells went off in my head. Greg and I then embarked on several years of medical opinions that failed to supply answers, apart from implying that we were bad parents. This hurt to the core. My argument was always that if his bizarre behaviour was my fault, why were the girls not like him?

Jenny Reid had worked with disabled children and told us, "Hayes appears to show traits of autism spectrum disorder." This was double Dutch to us; we had no idea what she meant. Our family doctor said, "There's something not right with your kid. You know that, don't you?" These were the only two people who were honest with us and did not try to blame us for being bad parents.

By the time Hayes was three, they had come up with a diagnosis: extreme attention deficit hyperactivity disorder (ADHD). He was too little for any medication to be prescribed, so we had to put up with him waking up every two hours during the night and running through the house. It was like having jet lag all the time.

It was not until he was four that a book on autism happened to be on the library shelf next to one on ADHD. I picked it up and was shocked: there was a list of symptoms on the inside cover and Hayes had most of the indicators to be on the autistic spectrum. Jenny had been right.

On visiting an expert and paying $250 we finally got a report that confirmed this. I was told by one honest doctor, "No one likes to be the one to give the 'A' word to a parent." This wasn't much help: because we hadn't known what was wrong, we had been denied the benefits of early intervention. Hayes had suffered two brain haemorrhages when he was born due to his prematurity. I still think this has contributed to his autism.

Another diagnosis was that Hayes, who was like a two-year-old in a four-year-old's body, suffered from 'global delay': a politically correct word for 'retarded'. People cringe when I use that word, but I think it is very descriptive. There is no beating around the bush. An autistic child will be an autistic adult. A delayed child will be a delayed adult. Yes, miracles do happen and I have seen many. As a parent you must never lose hope, but I like to know the truth, so I can face it.

At the age of seven, our little boy has been diagnosed with severe ADHD, moderate to severe autism and global delay. He only got out of nappies at the age of six, and is still known to finger paint the walls with poo. All our windows are meshed on the inside as he is a self-harmer, and the lights have been recessed into the ceiling. Hayes has no sense of danger and little spontaneous speech. He parrots phrases like, "Chippies for Hayes," or "Go to the park."

All the dreams we had for him are shattered. He goes on a special bus every day to a locked room in a school for intellectually disabled children. He will be there until he is eighteen. Luckily this is a fantastic facility with very special, dedicated staff. Hayes loves school and doesn't know any different. He also loves riding his tricycle around and going for swims. The pupils go on excursions to the shops and McDonalds to practise their social skills. Our main concern is that he is happy.

The fact that Hayes has such high needs has been very hard on all the family. We have to balance all the time he takes, as someone has to shadow him constantly, and the needs of the girls. They have to experience some normality. Yet my nightmares are filled with dread for Hayes' future. How do we know he will continue to be looked after as well as he is now when Greg and I are no longer around? There are many parents who would roll over in their graves if they knew the institutions they had put their children into had been closed "for their own good". And now many people with intellectual disabilities are in poorly run programs, in gaol or even on the streets, not able to look after themselves because the government spends so little on caring for the mentally ill.

I spent several years blaming myself for Hayes' medical condition. Then I became angry about what the police culture has done to me and to my family. I'm convinced that Hayes' problems are partly due to his premature birth, and to the stress I suffered through the whole period of the Royal Commission. This also applies to Bronte. I was very ill with a stress-related low functioning immune system that led to complications resulting in her premature birth. I can come to grips with what the police have done to me over the years, but not with the disadvantages all my children have suffered.

During these hard years while Hayes and Bronte were young we were on our own. I didn't think it could get any worse, then Bronte started behaving like her big brother. She was more feral even than Hayes at times. *Oh no*, I thought. *Not two autistic kids.*

Hayes and Bronte started going to a special needs playgroup. Hayes really enjoyed the music part of it, though it was very hard to keep the two of them under control. As hard as playgroup was, it was the highlight of the week.

They then started going to a special preschool together, but I had to take Hayes away eventually. The woman running the school refused to admit that he had autism. She actually told me, "Debbie, if you were firmer with him he would stop this bad behaviour." The last straw came one morning while Hayes was examining the wall-mounted red fire extinguisher. As he touched the handle she slapped his hand. Mouth open, I stood there.

"He has to learn," she said, matter-of-factly. "He won't touch it again." That afternoon when I came to pick Hayes up he was playing with the red fire extinguisher as if he had not moved from that spot all day.

That was his last day at that preschool. I should have walked straight out with both my kids after giving that woman a piece of my mind. At least I did get them both away from an unhealthy environment.

Hayes had been accepted for a school for autistic children at Forestville. He did not stay there very long; the car trip each way was too much. He would try and jump out of the car at every possible opportunity, which made the journey too dangerous. What was the point of giving him the best education if he didn't survive it? Greg and I then decided to place him into a local school for intellectually disabled children, as it was more important that he was happy and not under pressure. He will reach his full potential in his own time.

When the new Fraud Enforcement Agency was set up in place of the Fraud Squad on 1 July 1994, most of the staff were told to find new positions elsewhere. Only a handful was moved to the new section. We thought the signs were good; Greg, being an honest and capable police officer, would surely be a candidate for promotion. But when he applied he was passed over in favour of younger, less experienced police who had never been involved in fraud investigations. This was a huge smack in the mouth, the final blow. After this happened twice he never applied for another position again.

I knew how this worked: if they couldn't get me, the next target was Greg. They had to make an example of him to any others who might think about speaking out. In doing so, they made his life a living hell. As well as being stopped in his career path, Greg was socially isolated and ostracised. Subtle threats would be conveyed as jokes, or everyone would get up and walk out of the room when he entered.

Greg had been officially diagnosed with post-traumatic stress disorder in 1996, yet he was being placed under more and more pressure. He fought for a long time not to go off sick with anxiety and depression. He needed medication at times just to function. Even though Greg should have gone for a pension when I did and got out for his own safety and wellbeing, he just couldn't. He was also like me in that he lived and breathed being a cop and couldn't imagine life not in the job. Most police are like that; being a cop is a lifestyle career. Quite a few leave and rejoin because they miss it so much.

Greg is the most patient, gentle person I have ever known. I have never seen him lose his temper, even under the greatest provocation. Yet in 2001 he snapped. He was in the Drug Squad, doing very dangerous, stressful work that often required him to do twenty-four-hour shifts investigating clandestine drug laboratories. At home on the morning of 5 May, suffering from exhaustion after having worked all the previous day and through the night, he put his fist through a glass door panel in frustration. Blood gushed onto the timber floor from a deep slash across his right forearm.

After he had been in surgery for three and a half hours I was informed that he had severed his median nerve, artery and six tendons. He has some movement in his right hand now, but it is partially numb, which makes it very difficult to do fine work, such as writing or doing up buttons – let alone doing anything like using a handgun.

In 2002 he was designated Hurt on Duty by the Police Department, not because of the accident and its consequences but because of the stress he was placed under by his superior officers. After twenty years, he had to throw in the towel. All he wanted to be is a cop, and they just wouldn't let him do his job.

The last few years have seen a lot of painful changes, with the ripples from the Royal Commission causing unrest in many quarters. Yet many corrupt rats have deserted the sinking ship. That's got to be good for New South Wales. Some commentators and elements of the media have been highly critical of the former Commissioner Peter Ryan, yet people forget that Operation Florida, set up to investigate corruption, was a long-term investigation that wasn't leaked back to those under suspicion.

In April 2002, I was asked to represent Dr Jean Lennane at the Internal Witness Advisory Council, set up as a result of the Royal Commission to discuss and implement policy regarding police whistleblowers. It was chaired by the Commissioner of Police with the commanders of Internal Affairs and the Internal Witness Support Unit present, as well as representatives from ICAC, the ombudsman's office and the community. I accepted the request because I thought that with my experiences as a whistleblower I could do some good, and perhaps also because I was longing to walk into Police Headquarters again.

Running late to the meeting on Friday 26 April, I arrived in front of the building, looking around to see if I recognised anybody. Things had changed since last I was there, including the security. Now I had to fill out a form and wear identification. Glass partitions prevented unauthorised access to the lifts. I was even escorted by a security guard up to the seventeenth floor.

Although the foyer had been brought up to speed, upstairs was the same old drab 1970s interior with the basic office furniture. The view, however, is just breathtaking when you get up that high. Sydney surely is a beautiful city.

Much of the meeting referred to surveys being conducted to demonstrate that the police were doing a fine job. But things livened up when I asked, "What about the seven hundred and twenty police off on long-term stress leave, compared to the seven they had six years ago?"

At this, the boss of Internal Affairs Brian Reith went red in the face, which made for a great contrast to his white hair.

"Why do so many police leave and go off with stress?" I pressed on. "It is very expensive to train new members, and you can't put old heads on young shoulders."

"Seventeen hundred are going through the Academy at the moment," I was told. "We are going to have a lot of new police on the street. The officers on stress have mainly been hurt and then get stressed when it takes so long to process their matters. I am looking into putting more of my people on to keep contact with ill staff."

"Can I make a suggestion?" I continued. "An extensive debriefing program prior to police leaving would be helpful in showing where improvements could be made. Also, many may leave due to the police culture."

"Come on Debbie," exploded Brian Reith. "What are you going on about?"

"I'm not here to cause trouble. This is a forum on whistleblowing. I'm throwing ideas around for brainstorming that may help in dealing with police."

I might as well have saved my breath. Nobody was interested in what I had to say. I came to the realisation that I did not have the patience to deal with them any longer. I realised I could talk to them till I was blue in the face, but they didn't want to hear what I was saying. From that moment, I was free of them for good.

Although times have been tough, the future is looking brighter. I am optimistic and full of hope. Most importantly, this whole experience has not left me bitter. Along the way I have found strong and dependable people who have supported me, including the many doctors and psychologists who have treated me, as well as Greg and the kids. Greg has been my rock, without him I could not have kept going at times. Fantastic people have also given us support and kindness in relation to Hayes.

On 18 May 2002 Greg and I held a large celebration with the people who have helped and supported us over the last twelve years. It was a delight that we were still standing after what we'd been through. It was also to mark a new beginning and a closure to the past. I had told Greg on our wedding day that we would do it all again in ten years' time (get married again, that is) and we did. This time I felt really good about the celebration and kept singing the Elton John song, "I'm still standing, yeah yeah yeah."

Being older and wiser now, would I have done anything differently? Probably not. People avoid the truth but I was never destined to be a sheep. If I could change anything it would be the damage Hayes has sustained.

I've been told that I am one of the few success stories in whistleblowing. Maybe this is because I didn't let them beat me while always keeping sight of the big picture. I travelled my journey one day at a time, otherwise it would have been too overwhelming. Maybe because I am a recovering alcoholic, this was one of the things that helped me survive; following a spiritual recovery program gave me the living skills to endure the most difficult circumstances.

Alcoholics Anonymous has a twelve-step program as a basic plan for living. The first few steps are about accepting that you are powerless over that first drink, then it goes on to look at the past. When the damage is examined, you need to view your part in it and make amends to people you have harmed. It ends up with prayer and meditation and passing the word on to other alcoholics who are still suffering. This is big stuff. The steps are a plan for living that my biological family was not capable of giving me. They were also victims who had come from the same dysfunctional family. The only difference between my parents and me is that I decided the life I was leading wasn't good enough. I chose to live a better way.

You wouldn't think someone would be glad to be an alcoholic, but I am now. I loved to drink because it blotted out the pain and helped me escape from the reality of life. Unfortunately, reality would hit me in the face the next morning. I wouldn't have survived back then if I hadn't been a drinker, yet I am very lucky to have come into the rooms of AA at such a young age. Thank God my kids have never seen me drink.

I live by the AA serenity prayer, which goes:

God grant me the serenity
To accept the things I cannot change
Courage to change the things I can
And the wisdom to know the difference

Today I embrace my past. What doesn't kill you makes you stronger and if I hadn't had such a hard journey I would not appreciate what I have now. I am healing on my journey of recovery.

In 2002 a friend, Susan Reid, and I started up an autism and Asperger's syndrome support group. Her son Brodie is the only boy I've known who even comes close to Hayes in terms of energy. Sue and her husband had been dying of isolation in the suburbs too, but we discovered we lived only five minutes away from each other. We now have a large group, giving support and information to other families in the inner western suburbs of Sydney. We have found that the parents of disabled children are more likely to understand our problems than are other parents. Many of our old friends have been spooked by Hayes and not wanted him near their children or in their homes. Autism is not contagious.

I was wrong to think that I was finished with the police: they had one last shock for me.

On 28 June 2003 I received a telephone call from my psychiatrist Dr Jean Lennane. "Deb, I need you to come in today," she said. "I have something I have to talk to you about." I couldn't imagine what she meant.

In her office, she handed me a padded postal envelope. I opened it, and discovered that I held a framed certificate in my hands. I had to read it a second time for it to sink in:

COMMISSIONER'S CERTIFICATE OF MERIT
awarded to
DEBORAH LEE LOCKE
In recognition of her ethical actions when bringing under notice police misconduct in 1989. Her subsequent efforts to report police corruption and mismanagement were instrumental in moves to establish the NSW Police Royal Commission. Former Constable Locke conducted herself with integrity and her important contribution to the subsequent police reform process is acknowledged. By her actions former Constable Locke displayed good work worthy of recognition and is awarded this Certificate of Merit.

This had been a long time in coming. I never really expected the Police Department to acknowledge my part in helping to bring about changes. Even in this book I cannot even fully describe the hell I endured for years, or the treatment Greg endured for being my husband. Tears came when I realised Irene and John should have been here to see this. After all their yelling at me for standing up to corruption, the journey that started in 1989 had finally been completed in 2003.

My God, it was hard. This piece of paper signed by Commissioner Ken Moroney means so much to me. It means recognition, at last, that what I did was right. I spent so many years feeling I had done the wrong thing, and was continually punished for my actions.

With my certificate was a letter signed by Commissioner Moroney stating that, 'Due to privacy requirements, I am not in a position to ascertain the current address of Deborah Locke. I would request your assistance in forwarding this certificate to the former member.'

Recipients of awards are usually given the choice of a public or private presentation with a handshake from the commissioner or his representative. Having received this award, I would be proud to have it presented publicly. It would also be of benefit for young police to witness integrity and determination rewarded. Let's hope I am down at Goulburn soon for a passing out parade of new constables to receive my pat on the back and give inspiration to young recruits not to be bullied by the culture.

My losses have been great, yet I am also stronger. I am sober and have my own beautiful family of Greg, Vanessa, Hayes and Bronte, as well as being surrounded by warm and supportive friends. Having started with nothing, today I feel my life has been truly enriched.

I hope my story might be an inspiration to others that no matter how bad things get, or how impossible the odds seem, keep fighting the good fight. Keep it simple and just do it one day at a time.